# Opening A Dental Practice

# Opening A Dental Practice

by
R.H. Schaper, D.D.S.

**PennWell Books**

DENTAL ECONOMICS

**PennWell Publishing Company**
Tulsa, Oklahoma

Copyright © 1996 by
Pennwell Publishing Company
1421 South Sheridan/P.O. Box 1260
Tulsa, Oklahoma 74101

Schaper, R. H.
Opening a dental practice/R.H. Schaper
p.   cm.
Includes bibliographical references and index.
ISBN 0-87814-590-7
1. Dentistry—Practice.   I. Title
[DNLM: 1. Practice Management, Dental.   2. Private Practice—organization & administration. WU 77 S299o 1996]
RK58.S3643  1996
617.6'0068—dc20
DNLM/DLC
for Library of Congress                                                                    96-12933
                                                                                              CIP

All rights reserved. No part of this book may be reproduced, stored in a retrieval system, or transcribed in any form or by any means, electronic or mechanical, including photocopying and recording, without the prior written permission of the publisher.

Printed in the United States of America
1  2  3  4  5  00  99  98  97  96

# Dedication

This book is dedicated
to the memory of

Grace Ann,

who had the unswerving
conviction I could always be better
than I was.

# CONTENTS

Introduction ix

1. *Do You Belong In Private Practice?*     *1*
2. *Location, A General Overview*     *11*
3. *Narrowing Your Selection Down*     *23*
4. *Double Checking Your Choice*     *35*
5. *Scoping Out Your Potential Competition*     *41*
6. *Buy, Build, Or Lease?*     *47*
7. *Nailing Down The Ideal Office*     *53*
8. *Purchasing A Practice*     *67*
9. *Evaluating A Practice, General Considerations*     *79*
10. *The Expense Side Of The Ledger Sheet*     *91*
11. *The Patient Files*     *97*
12. *Deciding If A Practice Is Reasonably Priced*     *103*
13. *Financing*     *119*
14. *Notes On Negotiating The Purchase*     *129*
15. *The Partnership, Association Leading To Partnership And/Or Eventual Buyout*     *135*

| | |
|---|---|
| 16. *Space Sharing* | *141* |
| 17. *Involvement With Managed Care* | *149* |
| 18. *Structuring Fees And Analyzing Them For Profitability* | *165* |
| 19. *A Checklist* | *175* |
| 20. *Conclusions* | *179* |
| *Appendix 1: Basic Data Needed to Analyze a Practice* | *181* |
| *Appendix 2: Questions To Ask Yourself* | *189* |
| *Appendix 3: Suggested Reading* | *211* |
| *Appendix 4: State and Regional Board Information* | *213* |

# Acknowledgements

Though my name appears on the cover, I didn't actually write this book. Dozens of other dentists did. I merely compiled their combined unpleasant experiences. To all of these dedicated, but sometimes naive, professionals, I give thanks.

Then there's my own family and friends who put up with my moaning while I labored. To list them all would add several boring pages. Just know your suffering forbearance is recognized!

There's the assistance of the ADA librarians. They managed without exception to translate my bumbling generic requests for assistance into pertinent material. Without them several chapters would have been impossible.

At least three people at PennWell deserve accolades. Mr. Dick Hale, editor of Dental Economics, has been constantly supportive of everything I've written. I'm doubly grateful for his allowing me to use material contained in the chapter on fees. Ms. Sue Rhodes Sesso, dental market manager, has been wonderful from the moment I first contacted her. The third is Mr. Kirk Bjornsgaard, dental products editor. His comments and suggestions added materially to the content, quality, and scope of this book. To these three and all the others at PennWell who have labored in my behalf, thank you sincerely for putting up with me!

Equal thanks go to Mrs. Amber Heffington, who saved me from several weeks of frustration when time was critical.

Finally, a special nod to Dr. Bob Ackerman. His requests for advice and counsel sparked the idea for this book. Later his comments on the content were appreciated. Thanks, Bob!

# Introduction

We dentists are an independent lot. It's almost axiomatic to say every young (and sometimes not so young) dentist wants to be his or her own boss.

The thrill of being able to practice the way we wish, to "do our own thing," is ingrained in most of us. It eventually becomes an obsession for nearly all of us from the day we enter dental college. I can attest to the fact it's an exhilarating feeling to be the master of your own professional fate.

This yearning eventually has us looking through commercial "For Rent" ads or pestering obliging practice brokers for details on the "perfect" practice.

Those of us who've been through the travail of opening that first office regretfully, in retrospect, recognize we were woefully unprepared for what sometimes ended up an ordeal. There were no illustrated guide books or Rand McNally pocket maps to steer us past the myriad of pot holes and detours scattered along the way.

Which is why this book has been written. It has a dual purpose. The first is to point you in the direction of making rational decisions, as opposed to emotional ones which may lead to trouble. The second is to alert you to the existence of those aforementioned pot holes which may appear no matter how rational you are.

I'll outline the procedures you should use to keep you on track, no matter what you run into. But remember, the final choices must be yours. Remember, too, many of your decisions will be, at best, partially emotional. For example, you'll undoubtedly avoid Florida if you off-hour passion is centered on a ski slope. You'll probably shun a big city if you hate rush hour traffic and are allergic to the resulting smog. There are often family considerations. I'll help you put these things in perspective as we go along.

However, these necessary basic emotional tugs must be overlaid with a bit of common sense and a lot of hard business planning if you're to minimize the risk of going down in defeat.

It may come as a shock to the neophyte to learn dentists are capable of going broke. It's no secret most new commercial ventures fail. Risk is there. Even for us. Your degree is no guarantee of financial security even though far fewer dental practices fail than is the norm for all small businesses. It's my intent to change the statistics in favor of the professional!

It will serve you well to remember the biggest reasons for those disasters are a failure to develop a sound business appraisal and a disregard for intensive initial planning.

There will be no hard dollar values given, since what would be valid as this is being written may be obsolete by the time the printing process is completed.

What I will give you are sufficiently detailed reasonably acceptable guidelines and alternatives so you'll be able to apply some basic business principles to your unique situation. Let me stress, and stress again and again: All decisions must be up to you, for if you try to rely totally on me (or any other so-called expert), the resulting office and/or practice won't be yours, it'll be ours. That might lead to some financial success. Others made it work, didn't they? But if your own stamp isn't on the practice, it's for sure you would end up a miserable, emotional basket case.

From time to time you'll also find a bit of historical perspective on private practice. There's a sneaky reason for this. Too often we dentists forget there are long-term trends that must not be ignored lest we find ourselves bucking an unstoppable tide.

The living history of an older practitioner may read like an ancient myth to the recent graduate, but only by knowing where we've been as a profession can we have any chance of predicting where we're collectively going. That's vital if you expect to succeed as an entrepreneur—for as the profession goes, so must you. That is, if you wish to succeed financially.

I urge you to remember as you peruse the various separate topics that they're all intimately interrelated. Choosing a location has a distinct bearing on a decision to purchase or to pass on an available practice that's for sale. Financing requirements, whether you open your own office or buy one, directly affect a decision as to the type of equipment you purchase or lease. It may dictate whether you purchase or lease. Your own outlook on the way you would like to dispense your expertise will have an impact on the extent to which you seek out and participate in alternative practice modalities. This in turn may greatly influence the location you choose.

Though you'll look long and hard to find any reference to it in conventional books on practice management, each and every detail of a completely successful office is closely integrated. The fee schedule is tied into the selection of reception room furniture. This decor in turn is tied into the

## Introduction

marketing strategy.

All these factors have a bearing on the personnel the doctor hires—and even to the uniforms those assistants wear. I can even make a reasonably good argument that those same uniforms can have an effect on, or be affected by, the hours the office is open!

Because of this intertwining, you'll find a number of intentional redundancies in the pages that follow. For example, the subject of fees is germane to the purchase of a practice. So is financing. Therefore, fees are taken seriously when discussing the purchase of a practice.

You'll find references to overhead in many spots, sometimes using similar examples to make different points. Please don't try to isolate one aspect of entering private practice from all the rest. That's a formula for failure!

There's a plethora of detail concerning location. It's intentional. Here's why.

The location you select dictates most of the other decisions you'll make down the line. Some of these effects are highlighted to increase your awareness of this intertwining. I urge you to use them—and the questions section in the appendix—to guide your thinking about precisely what sort of practice will make you happiest.

A number of subjects are treated with a more "overview" approach. For example, the advice is more general on a topic such as leasing terms. Here it's more necessary and prudent for you to consult with a specific expert. In this instance, an attorney. In these spots I've paid definite attention to helping you sort through those experts to find one who will sincerely look out for your interests as opposed to someone who will only want to empty your pocket.

Burn it into your brain, however, that even though a particular topic is not dealt with in exquisite detail, it doesn't mean it's not crucial to your success! If you feel you need more detailed information than is possible to compress into a book of this sort, I urge you in the strongest possible terms to explore and profit from all available sources of wisdom. To aid you in this endeavor, a few relevant books are listed in the appendix. Seek out and absorb them—and others as well!

Regrettably, there's one important subject you may find obsolete by the time this book is published. That's managed care. I finished that particular chapter last and already new facets of the subject are appearing. Like me, you'll soon see new variations of the basic schemes being hatched continuously and old ones falling out of favor at about the same rate.

As detailed in that chapter, this is due to the government, insurance companies, and employers constantly jockeying for a better position in the financial dance of cost containment. I'll teach you some of the basic steps!

To help you cope with this type of constantly shifting situation, you'll see there's a chapter on fees. It's useful for more than merely analyzing a fee schedule. It'll provide you with the means to do the hard numbers for your practice so that you can decide if, and possibly to what extent, you should join one of the alphabet organizations.

A couple of words of explanation about the approach I've used in imparting information. You'll find the general tone of this book informal. It would be easy to make it conform to normal textbook standards by pompously using the more conventional third person designation of "the reader" and "the author" when referring to you and me. Frankly, I think it makes for cumbersome reading and detracts from the swift flow and clarity of information.

Finally, if this book does nothing more than make you stop and think rationally about the requirements for taking that giant step of striking out on your own, then it's been worth writing.

Please! Remember the many pitfalls pointed out are not highlighted with an intention of dashing your dreams! Far from it. Owning your own practice can be a wonderful and exciting adventure, full of gratification and pleasure.

For me, it would be most satisfying to feel you've gained significant insight into the process of locating and planning for the perfect practice—thereby increasing your chances of succeeding without more stress than necessary.

That is a mouthful, and probably more than should be wished for by even the most egotistic author. My more realistic hope is, you'll find a couple of things you might find useful; thus saving you at least one giant headache during this trying but emotionally exciting time when you're finally reaching for your professional dream.

# Chapter 1

# Do You Belong In Private Practice?

Perhaps this question should be rephrased to read:

Do you belong in your own solo private practice, as a co-owner of a group where some or all of the non-technical decisions are left to others, or should you be working for wages or commission for someone else?

Your answer is important. It's the first thing you should find out about yourself. Why? Because you do have a real choice.

Historically, philosophically, and culturally, all of us have been geared and programmed to believe there is only one honorable answer to that question: "Yes, running my own private practice is for me!"

Those of us who graduated some years ago had precious few alternative examples to base our decision on. The dentist who treated us when we were kids was in solo private practice. Our schools were (and to a great extent still are) geared to producing private practitioners—with the emphasis on solo. Our society has traditionally considered that to be the only way to go—if not immediately, then sometime in our professional career. It's not acceptably normal for us to think otherwise.

That's the historic concept of nearly all professions, and up until the last few years, it was about the only viable alternative for a graduate of a professional school. As recently as 40 years ago it was a radical concept for more than one dentist to practice under the same roof, much less enter a true partnership agreement. Even rarer was the "associate," a fancy term back then for an underpaid hired flunky.

Most of the exceptions were father-and-son offices where Junior was marking time and getting a little extra seasoning before Papa stepped aside. The practice was usually handed over as a belated graduation present or a premature inheritance for the younger generation.

Equally unusual was the idea of actually selling a practice. When a dentist retired, he simply junked his equipment, stuffed his files in the basement, and took a long trip. If he really cared about his patients he might drop them a note telling them he was out of business.

That meant nearly every graduate stepped out on his or her own before the ink on the diploma and license was no longer blottable. About the only viable alternative was to go back to the school that disgorged them into the cruel world and train more dentists to open offices. The few renegades who chose military service as a career or became institutional mouth-maulers were looked upon with suspicion by the rest of the profession. The feeling was they were deficient in some part of their personality or ability. Either that, or totally lacking in ambition.

What clinical research that was done was primarily carried out by general practitioners who had an idea and tried it out on their unsuspecting patients. Making a career out of research was almost unknown. A handful of dentists went to work as front men for toothpaste makers or lent their names to other proprietary oral products. Generally, these repugnancies were viewed as a tide-me-over until the individual had laid by enough cash to open that required office.

One or two graduates might even turn up as missionaries to some backward country. Even this laudable calling was whispered over with the suspicion that a psychiatrist should be called in for consultation.

The minority who made alternative career choices were more aberrations than exceptions to the rule. Their classmates shook their heads at reunions and quietly asked each other how these misfits ever got into dental school in the first place.

It's trite to say times have changed. There's currently a tremendous, fully acceptable latitude in the choices available to the new graduate. Most are considered honorable. In spite of this diversity, the perception persists that the ultimate landing strip is in a private practice where the owner is monarch of all he, and now she, surveys.

These alternatives are extremely fortunate, since the complexity of running a private practice has increased far beyond the worst indigestion-induced nightmares of our predecessors. What was once a one-person unfettered operation has transformed into a complex, highly-regulated business venture.

Let me stress the word "business." Today's practitioner must juggle intense governmental regulation, unremitting commercial insurance requirements and restrictions, fractious specialized ancillary personnel, and rising overhead requirements. Today's self-employed dentist delicately balances these obstacles while coping with increasing patient expectations and rapidly changing treatment modalities. A once-docile public who idolized the doctor as a minor god now considers him an adversary at times, questioning treatment recommendations and fees. Additionally, this same public routinely demands what often amounts to undeliverable results and gleefully sues when those demands aren't exceeded.

This means the individual in solo private practice has to be far more than a technically competent dentist with enough personality to attract a share of the market. Long gone are the days when the profession itself dictated the number of new entrants to its ranks in order to ensure all had a decent patient pool to draw from.

Private practice now demands, in addition to the traditional technical excellence a mix of personnel manager, that a dentist be an accounting wizard, purchasing agent, public relations expert, and hard headed business administrator. Today's dentist must be just as much at ease with the world of crass commerce as he or she is with a mouth mirror.

This vastly-changed climate makes the question at the head of the chapter a valid one, and one that any dentist thinking about opening an office must answer with self-searching candor. This objective self-appraisal is not easy!

One thing is reasonably certain. The new graduate has been well trained in the art and science of the profession, but has received minimal exposure to the rigors of the marketplace. For example, it often comes as a shock to the neophyte that dealing with a patient in a practice setting is surprisingly different from treating the clinic patient. Pleasing a critical professor by producing a perfect margin is a far cry from pleasing a critical patient who takes for granted the margin will be adequate.

This paying patient expects deference and appreciation for the dollars brought in the front door. At the same time, nearly every patient wants to look up to this despised servant as a superior in some weird Freudian way. Filling this strange dual role requires skills not covered in the curriculum that culminated in the graduation ceremony.

Because numerous viable and culturally-acceptable alternatives currently exist for short-term employment in an established office, I would urge the new graduate to seriously consider delaying striking out on his or her own.

The experience and insight gained through a period of indoctrination and adaptation at someone else's expense is well worth the delay in reaching for one's own goals.

This preparation pays in two ways. The experience gained makes stepping out into the cruel world a much easier task. Only through experience can anyone determine if he or she is actually suited to the changing demands of running an office. More than one disillusioned young doctor has come to the conclusion that private practice is not the best career choice, thus saving years of frustration and financial hardship.

Once insight is gained as to what owning a practice really means, it's time for a dose of realism as to whether you, as a duly licensed dentist, are truly suited for this option. Though it may have been your dream, the Norman Rockwell concept of a kindly practitioner leisurely dispensing aid and comfort without regard to overhead, governmental requirements, or other pesky intrusions is a lovely myth. Buying into that dream without understanding its consequences can lead to disaster.

One other advantage to a year or two of seasoning is learning what type of practice suits you. It isn't enough to say you want a private practice. In today's society you have to plan what niche you want.

Here's what I mean. You must learn whether you're cut out to handle a large volume of patients or are better off with a smaller, more intimate operation. Do you want a traditional fee-for-service arrangement or can you be successful contracting with one or more HMOs or other alphabet alternative modalities? What type of patient are you most comfortable with?

I repeat: The hard headed reality is, the practice of dentistry today is more of a business than it is a profession. The very reasons most of us entered the field initially tend to work against financial success in today's competitive environment. You, as a prospective practice owner, must realize there are times when choices must be made between the idealism so essential to a professional and the pragmatism demanded by financial considerations.

This leads to the first difficult specific question you should answer before you make any commitment. This self assessment test should be taken seriously. You might even find it helpful to write down the answers. You might also discuss what you've determined with a trusted friend who'll tell you the truth as to whether you're kidding yourself or not. (I would not generally recommend consulting a spouse! There's a good reason for the saying that love is blind.)

This first big basic question is: Will I be miserable if I must compromise even one professional standard I've set for myself?

Just in case you have any misunderstanding about the question, let me give you an example. Suppose your patient in your judgment requires two lower fixed bridges. It's the treatment you've been taught to deliver, and you've gained enough experience to agree it's the best choice for the particular situation. You file insurance papers and schedule an appointment to begin.

Back come the authorizations from the insurance company. They will allow for the placement of a removable partial denture, a much less expensive, and from their vantage point, a financially preferable alternative. You feel certain your patient will not make up the difference. You discover that no matter what the patient's been told, the group policy wording expressly mandates the less expensive alternative. What do you do?

You know an appeal to the insurance company's consultant will do no good. They've been inflexible before. Once a decision is made by one of the clerks, it sticks. You realistically have three viable choices: You can swallow your judgment whole and make the partial. You can refuse to continue any treatment. Or, you can absorb the extra cost. (Absorbing the extra cost means you either lose money or make practically nothing.)
What is your answer?

If it's any comfort to you, there's no correct solution to this personal dilemma. However, your answer may give you some insight as to how you might conduct that dream practice you're after. It may also be a predictor of the amount of financial success you'll have. It's redundant to point out only one of the possibilities listed above is financially sound.

The discomfort level you feel when considering a compromise of this sort may indicate how miserable you'll be in a practice where such decisions are an everyday occurrence. Without a decent comfort level, you're going to hate your practice in a short time. This could be hazardous to your mental health.

You may argue that decisions such as this one come up whether you're the boss or not. True, but it generally isn't your neck alone that's stuck out to the next county. You may not like a boss who overrides your professional judgment, but your integrity can remain reasonably intact in such a situation.

The next question you need to ask yourself is: How good a personnel manager will I be?

It's not like it once was. Grandpappy probably spent half his professional life alone in his office. No assistants, no receptionist, no hygienist, no in-house lab technician. Maybe if he was one of the more successful practitioners he hired a "girl" to answer the phone, throw instruments in boiling water, and mix amalgam. That was it. If the "girl" gave him any static, he fired her and found another.

It didn't matter much. It was a no-skill, minimum-wage job. The "girls" found it much preferable to clerking in the dime store, so there was usually a line waiting for the job. In the meantime his practice continued on an even course just about the same. What "girl" he had at the moment didn't add to or subtract much from the patient load.

Moreover, he didn't have unemployment paperwork, workman's compensation insurance or pension plans to worry about. He didn't have to bond his staff. Medical insurance wasn't ever considered. He gave them an extra ten spot at Christmas and got a grateful kiss on the cheek for his generosity!

It may have been idyllic. It definitely seems so today, but we all know running a practice like that sure won't work now. We've become totally dependent on ancillary personnel—and they know it! So, let's redefine the question along these lines:

Can you honestly say you're the type who's comfortable being the boss, understanding all the term implies?

Being a boss means screening applicants for a job; hiring judiciously; training efficiently; praising, disciplining, an *documenting* both the good and unacceptable behavior of your employees, firing someone when necessary; and being conversant with and adhering to all the arcane rules and regulations imposed on your business by various, occasionally conflicting, governmental bodies.

Being a boss means juggling work schedules when someone's sick, his or her kids are sick, or when and assistant shows up with a hangover. Being a boss means holding the lid down on inter-office petty jealousies. Being a boss means watching to make sure everyone does his or her fair share in the office. Being the boss means keeping a jaundiced eye on the cash register. Being the boss means you're responsible for constantly fitting into your operation all those new people you'll constantly have to hire.

Being a boss can seem like a full-time job in itself. It will be unless you're halfway good at it. So before you step out on your own, be sure you're equipped for this part of the job. Unsatisfactory employees will wreck your chances for success about as fast as anything imaginable.

The next personality trait you need to examine is a bit easier to assess, possibly because a negative answer is a bit more socially acceptable. It involves money management. Here it is: Can you manage money?

There's a trap hidden in that query. Most of us can take a limited budget and eke out a hamburger diet on it. We did it when we were in school. We usually managed to make our allowances work when we were kids. We've learned to keep our credit in fair shape and avoid having the finance company pick up our car in the middle of the night. So where's the problem?

Managing money in a dental practice is a bit different. There are long term decisions to be made, self denial when times are good, and purchasing options that would make the eyes of a Solomon swap sockets. Many practitioners duck this area of their practice by over-employing an accountant.

Relying on an accountant to dictate professional business decisions is one of the larger mistakes you can make. For example, the books may say you've depreciated a piece of equipment, so you should replace it. This may make narrow actuarial sense but it's an impractical way of doing business.

Here is a concrete example. The mere fact an X-ray machine is 10 years old doesn't mean it's ready for the junk heap. One of my colleagues has one machine that's been snapping candid shots of molars for 20 years. It passes all the governmental tests with perfection. It would be stupid of her to spend the price of a good cruise for the family just to change it out. There's only one problem. Twenty-year-old X-ray machines are entering the age when they may give out.

This doctor is faced with several choices. She could go ahead and buy the new X-ray machine. She could use the money to redecorate the office, thereby enhancing her appeal to both new and existing patients. Or, she could just let the cash allocated to the purchase of the new machine sit in the bank and accumulate interest. All are acceptable business decisions. What is best for this practice?

Be totally honest with yourself when you say you're equipped psychologically and emotionally to undertake this responsibility. A lot of people may get hurt if you aren't.

I've saved the rough bit of self-analysis for last. This question is the hardest to answer without resorting to self delusion. It involves digging deep into the depths of your soul. Nevertheless, it's one that must be asked: Do I have the personality traits needed to run a successful practice?

Here again, a comparison of what used to be and what's required today is useful. Until around 1980, the delivery of dental service was a seller's market. The ratio of available professionals to the demand of the public for treatment was favorable. Patients were far more willing to accept treatment simply because the dentist said it was necessary.

This translated into the happy security of knowing that merely having your name in the phone book was sufficient. Making a living didn't require much effort outside of diagnosis and treatment. You might or might not get rich, but you were bound to eat reasonably regularly.

Not today. Today's dentist operates in something of a demanding buyer's market. Dentists can—and do—go broke because of personality flaws which have nothing to do with their professional skills. They may have all the other requirements for success but lack the skill to relate properly to their patients. We seldom dramatically save lives—a powerful practice builder utilized by our medical brethren. We must, therefore, rely on our ability to coddle and nurture members of the great American public to keep them coming back to our office.

We must be salesmen! Little of what we do will materially alter the life span of our patients, so the patients must be sold on the idea that a lovely three-unit bridge will make life better and more rewarding. That's not easy when you're competing for the patient's disposable income with a ski weekend or the down payment on a shiny new automobile.

Some of these skills can be learned, some cannot. If you recognize potential deficiencies in your character that might make it more difficult to be successful, proceed with caution.

Since this is a generic book, one other note must be added for the women who've entered the profession. As a significant number of ladies graduating as dentists is a rather recent occurrence, a special word or two must be addressed to their special situation. I take it as a given that you ladies are at least as competent as your male counterparts—and probably a bit superior because of the innate prejudice you had to overcome to get your degree.

You will, unfortunately, have to fight that battle one more time as you enter your own private practice. If you're married, many traditionalists will view your practice as something you're doing as a hobby of sorts and not as a permanent or serious undertaking. If you're single, you may be viewed with suspicion by jealous wives as a predatory threat to their security. I assume you've already addressed the multiple problems associated with occasional premenstrual syndrome, the possibility of pregnancy, and motherhood vs. professional demands— all issues your future patients will gossip over.

Silly? Sure. Unfair? Sure. Unwarranted? Sure. Maddening? Definitely! But I've heard those sentiments expressed concerning a completely stable, happily married lady who had to work very hard to establish herself as a serious practitioner. This denigration regrettably included comments by a couple of her professional colleagues.

If you're single, you may have to alter your social life somewhat to initially overcome derogatory neighborhood back-fence gossip. For what it's worth, if you've come this far, you probably have it in you to make that final step leading you to great success.

If you have some other minority connotation, you may face equivalent difficulties. Unfortunately the world is not perfect and neither are its inhabitants. I can only remind you that some of the additional obstacles that may initially appear can often be turned into assets. They may even make your path to success a bit easier. Success may be no more than a matter of finding a slightly different path!

Let me emphasize once more that if you feel uncomfortable about any of your answers to the above self-appraisal quiz, you might do well to consider entering a practice arrangement which minimizes your involvement in a specific area. Alternatively, you may want to spend some time and effort strengthening these weaker aspects of your business abilities.

Knowing where your strengths and weaknesses are will materially assist you in entering that perfect practice that generates minimal stress. That'll make the private practice you're in a really rewarding pleasure instead of a chore. Certainly, if you feel you have the stuff to make your dream come true, go for it!

Above all, heed the lyrics of that old song: *Don't let the stars get in your eyes!* Don't let your dreams override common sense and level thinking about your options and your chances of success!

CHAPTER 2

# LOCATION, A GENERAL OVERVIEW

You're ready! You've spent enough time acquiring the additional technical and people skills you feel necessary to make it in private practice. You're comfortable discussing treatment and fees with patients. You're able to establish a rapport with people in an office setting. You've begun to chafe under the constraints of your present practice setting. You've assessed yourself and feel it's time to strike out on your own. It's time to start looking for your own place in the sun.

Or is it?

Before you run out and buy a map, *take time to know precisely what type of practice you want!* The following pages will give you particulars on finding the location to fit in with your projected practice scheme and plans. This part of the decision process is intensely personal, for only you can decide who you want for patients.

Knowing exactly the type of practice you're aiming for will make the site selection process much simpler. For that reason, you'll find a number of hints for each type of practice, and the best places to open your office for each.

This decision, as I said, is purely (or nearly purely) personal. There are teeth everywhere. There is office space available in every nook of this country. You're limited only by your own requirements and licenses. There are few, if any, spots in the land which are underserved as defined by the economics of the area. The financial leveling process has cleared the excess dental population out of those areas that were once thought of as the most desirable. In short, you can head anywhere you want.

So why do I devote so much space to the many aspects of location?

Any successful business owner will tell you location is one of the prime keys to success. Like it or not, dentistry is a business as well as a profession. Gone are the halcyon days when merely opening an office was a guarantee of patients.

People today demand more and expect more in the way of convenience and coddling than their parents or grandparents did. Added mobility and increased competition make it imperative you get a head start by picking the right spot to display your professional wares.

That means you have to make it as convenient as possible for the public you intend to woo to visit you. At the same time, you have to make it as comfortable for yourself as you can, otherwise you'll not be happy in your practice. If you're unhappy, your patients will sense that and draw back—maybe even to the office across the way.

A myriad of factors go into picking the right location. What's right for you may not be right for the classmate who sat in front of you in school. Your tastes are different, your backgrounds, and your expectations. Even the idea of how you want to practice will be unique to you.

Nevertheless, there are some general principles you should apply to any decision regarding a site to set up shop. Let's start with the non-economic ones first.

## PERSONAL AND EMOTIONAL DECISIONS

You probably have a pretty good idea already of what general type of community you want to settle in and the rough geographic location. Possibly you've already decided on exactly what zip code you wish to have on your address labels. Even so, it won't hurt to review a few of the factors that go into a wise choice. Feel free to add your own special criteria.

The requirement that comes to mind first is family. You can limit your considerations to no more than a spouse and/or any children you may have. You can, depending on your family structure, add parents, grandparents, and others. If you're indeed married, include the family crowd on both sides of the marital aisle. When considering family, it wouldn't be amiss to ask yourself if any of them now, or will in the foreseeable future, require special attention. Are you going to be the one responsible for handling that situation?

Obviously, you want a spot where your spouse will also be happy. If he or she wants to work, are there satisfactory opportunities for them? If both of you are working, whose job location takes precedence when there's a conflict?

If you have kids, they must be considered. For example, moving to a retirement community where they're the only under-age inhabitants for miles can be a real drag for everyone. Schools are an important thing, too. There are wide variations in quality from state to state and inside a state. There can even be significant variables within a community setting, depending on the school district structure. If you want the best for your offspring, don't forget to include their needs in your planning. The extended family is an equal consideration in many situations other than the one just mentioned. You might want to have your mother-in-law handy just down the street to act as a permanent volunteer baby sitter. Or you might want her a thousand miles or so away in order to keep peace in your own household. Possibly, you're responsible for providing part-time support or intermittent care for a chronically-ill relative. These all play a part in your choice, so factor them in.

Your off-duty needs must be considered, too. Man does not live by bread and peanut butter alone. You'll spend many more hours outside your office than you will in. Better have a climate you like. When I say climate, I mean far more than just the temperature and humidity, although you should take them into serious account. If, like me, you hate the thought of a snow shovel, look at somewhere other than an Alaskan mountain top village for your permanent residence.

Ask yourself seriously if you relish the bustle and exciting pace of the city, or do you prefer the more laid-back atmosphere of a small town. Do you require a choice of prepackaged entertainment always at your beck and call or are you happier with do-it-yourself pursuits? You may prefer opera or tractor pulls as great diversion for a night out—it doesn't matter. What matters is your satisfaction level.

Your fullest range of choices may be limited by the state board or boards you have under your belt. This can be frustrating if you want to make a long distance jump, but fortunately many of the prejudicially artificial restrictions states once placed on out-of-state applicants for their licensure exams have been removed.

Most competent dentists can now pass almost any board if they prepare themselves. But it's still a big hassle and you may not want to fight the system. Obtaining a license at the opposite end of the country is still a time-consuming and expensive process. It's up to you to decide how much you wish to compromise your wishes when stacked up against the realities you face.

If you do want to go for a different board, I've included a list of addresses for the various boards in the appendix. They'll give you particulars on where and when they test. Incidentally, there are several states which will license you under certain circumstances without taking a test. If you're interested in a particular spot, by all means ask.

A word of warning is due. I am acquainted with one unhappy dentist who is absolutely nuts over the game of golf. He'd play eight hours a day, every day of the year, if he could. He went to school in a northern state and passed the board there. After a couple of years, he decided the South provided a better climate which would allow him to swing a club almost 12 months a year. He reasoned this beat the measly four to six months his current location allowed.

He had no limiting responsibilities to deter him, so he took a new board. He passed and immediately moved South— into the heart of one of the most depressed areas of the country. All he looked at were the area's golf courses! He has plenty of time to play his beloved game, but can't make enough to afford the green fees!

The point? Don't let the stardust build up in your eyes so much you can't see anything else but that one dimension you think is all important. Check everything before you leap toward the unknown. You need more than agreeable surroundings to make it in this profession.

And that is the perfect place to begin to address more than the emotional side of making a choice of location. The next step is to factor in the financial part of the equation.

**ECONOMIC CONSIDERATIONS**

Few of us are as headstrong as my golf nut. We do a bit of investigating before we jump. Typically, we superficially look at a location, like what we see on the surface, and proceed to act on little more than impulse. More often than not, choosing that perfect location is more a matter of luck than true hard-headed business sense.

For many of us, that investigation begins with venerable ADA pamphlets designed to statistically assist in choosing a location. I ordered one years ago and used the information to confirm my feelings about a city I was sure was my ideal.

I fell flat on my face! In retrospect, the ADA information proved useless. The last edition of the same publication I saw a couple of years ago was no better. I'll grant all the statistics were accurate if not completely current, but they don't begin to tell the story.

Admittedly, the ADA has come up with more detailed information than they had back then. By all means, obtain all of it. If there's one axiom that holds true in setting up an office, it's that you never can have too much information. If you're a member, most of the literature's free. If you aren't (and shame on you), the cost is well worth it.

The next place a lot of us headed for was the local Chamber of Commerce. Avoid that trap like a middle ages plague! Most Chambers are in the deadly serious business of soundly promoting their area. Trumpeting even the smallest negative is the last thing they'll do. What you need is a decent library and a stout pair of walking shoes. Or a full tank of gas in your car. In other words, do your own research!

How do you start? By asking the right questions. Here are a few that should put you on track in assessing your prospective state, region, town, and neighborhood. I've included the reasons behind the queries so you can assess their importance to your particular situation

What is the tax structure and effective rate of the state and city you're looking at? It's no secret business goes where the tax treatment is most favorable. If taxes are excessive, business will go elsewhere when it wants to expand or cut costs. That translates into jobs gained or lost. Jobs are held by people, a tooth-bearing commodity you can't do without.

What is the economic base of the area? Real stability is a desirable thing to have in any community. It makes projecting your chances of getting ahead a lot easier.

For example, there are a number of southern communities which depend heavily on retirees for capital inflow. The checks these folks receive are predictable and fairly constant even in relatively turbulent economic times.

Contrast that with some of the farm state problems a few years ago. Farmers were hit with a triple whammy of poor weather, rising interest rates and unfavorable debt ratios. Large numbers of very good people went bankrupt. This may not have wiped out a batch of our colleagues, but it definitely didn't help their retirement accounts. For the beginning practitioner who's undertaken a mighty debt load to go into business, an economic downturn of this magnitude could be financially fatal.

The same situation may exist in "manufacturing" towns, especially smaller "company" communities where one industry dominates the economy. These places have spawned terms like "rust belt" and "job flight" which have crept into our language. Admittedly there is no way of accurately predicting the future, but an acute awareness of both global trends and changing local economic times is warranted when you're starting out.

It's no secret that currently, older somewhat staid industries are feeling a big pinch. So are their communities. Few of these cities and towns will disappear from the face of the Earth, but the boom times lost when a large industry or company moves out may take years to return. New companies, new policies, new innovations take time to implement. Be sure you have what it takes to weather that storm if it hits your location.

A suggestion. If possible, try and avoid a one-employer town. Here's an example.

As I write this, the defense department is in the throes of closing military bases all over the country. There are dozens of communities which have grown up around these facilities and exist almost solely on the paychecks of service personnel. The screams of economic pain being emitted by these folks are real. Dentists are affected right along with everybody else.

The next thing to check is whether the area you're looking at is growing, sitting still, or shrinking. When new people move into a spot to live and work, they have no ties with an existing practitioner. This means you have a better chance at getting your share of those patients. That's a lot easier than luring them away from someone else!

In a stable population the job is a bit more difficult. As I just said, you must essentially take patients away from some of the older established colleagues. I assure you your fellow professionals won't give paying patrons up without a fight. They have their own futures to think about.

In the shrinking economy, it gets really tough. Almost daily you can hear a television newscaster muttering something about a plant closing and laying off hundreds of workers. By the time that filters through whatever community is the target, several thousand others will also be looking for new jobs. That translates into the patient base equivalent of at least two average dental practices. In a city of 1 million people, this is hardly noticeable. In a town of 40,000 people, it's a disaster for everyone. It's worst if you're the new kid on the block.

### THE PAY SCALE FACTOR

Another thing that's important is the wage structure in the community and surrounding trade area. You should already know that no matter how necessary you may think your services are to the welfare of the patient, the patient often has other priorities.

People have a finite amount of disposable income to spread over several items on their wish lists. The more disposable income they have, the more likely they are to accept the complete, and professionally profitable, treatment recommendations you make.

The single lady raising a couple of kids, beating her brains out for little more than minimum wage, will simply not have the cash in the foreseeable future for that fancy crown you suggest. In fact, she may not even come in at all for more than emergency treatment because she knows she won't be able to pay the bill.

Wages do vary widely in this country. A classic example recently cited concerns auto assembly plants. The statistics were reported for 1994 and are used for comparison purposes only.

In Detroit, the average wage of an auto assembly plant worker is reported to be around $40.00 an hour including benefits. In South Carolina, that same worker, doing the same job, is costed out by the manufacturer at about $15.00. Even if both bring in the same insurance papers, the Detroit worker's family is in a better position to handle the co-payment and deductible simply because there is more money left after taking care of the necessities of life.

On the flip side, if the bosses have to close one of the two plants, do you want to guess which one it'll be? This points up the difficulty in being too sure of the future.

Another thing to look for is the education level of the people you'll be dealing with as patients. There are two reasons to consider this facet of your target patient pool.

The first is so obvious I hate to mention it. The more educated a person is, the more likely he or she is to have a better paying job. This means more disposable income for you to tap into.

The second is also obvious, but not so blaring as the first reason. The better educated your prospective patients are, the more conscious they are about good dental health. Whether this has anything to do with the economic edge education brings is undetermined, but it is a good possibility.

That is not to say you can't make a darned good practice out of pure emergency treatment—what I once heard referred to as "lunch bucket" dentistry. It merely requires a different approach than the one you're probably accustomed to and initially trained for. If you head into a high volume situation, be prepared to spend a lot of hours on roller skates going from treatment room to treatment room. You may already know what I mean if you've spent time laboring in some of the HMO clinics currently operating.

## DEMOGRAPHIC CONSIDERATIONS

Another way of looking at a prospective site is to consider the population age mix you're expecting to deal with and the relative advantages and disadvantages of each group. Let's start with the young adult set.

By and large, these are people struggling to get established. They're either just into their first home or working hard to get to that stage. They're buying furniture, cars, and having babies. Their debt level is high. Their parents probably sent them out into the world with a mouth in fine shape and they haven't had enough time to undo all those good works. You, my friend, are not high on their priority list. Equally unfavorable is the fact they're still not too far up the economic ladder as a group. They aren't all that secure in their jobs. A disproportionate part of their truly disposable income goes for entertainment.

On the plus side, you'll probably see a lot of small children and thus work the parents into your practice in time. Just be sure you have a large enough potential patient pool to deal with. Don't be in too much of a rush to make a killing. As these patients mature and increase their income, so will you.

Be prepared for a comparatively high turnover rate with these people. As their income grows and their family expands, they may very well move to a more affluent neighborhood. You'll have to work a little harder to keep them as patients after that.

For this type of practice, it's ideal to have your office sitting between that "starter" subdivision and one that features homes catering to those on the next rung of the ladder.

While I've classified the younger adults into a rather homogeneous grouping, the somewhat more mature patient pool has a number of subdivisions. The first is comprised of those a few years older than the young adults.

These people have probably moved into somewhat larger houses to accommodate their growing families. Either that, or they wish to enjoy the extra luxury a larger home provides. Their kids are in school, somewhere below the high school level. They've had a promotion or two and have begun to save a little money now and then. Though their expenses are higher than the younger set, their income has more than matched this increase. As a group, they're better money managers.

For them, the beginning dental ravages of time have begun to creep in. Things like minor gum problems, an occasional cracked tooth, worn out fillings, and the diminishing effects of those early fluoride treatments are showing up. With these people, the number in the available patient pool can be smaller. Moreover, they're becoming more conscious of their health and will follow your recommendations fairly closely. You'll also see a lot of their kids on the way to the orthodontist.

A warning. This group should be split into economic strata when planning on moving in amongst them. Many of those who haven't gone onward and upward in the corporate structure may be putting on a darned good front while eating beans five times a week. Those toiling for a modest hourly wage may even be taking pay cuts in order to keep their jobs. Even if they haven't, their pay checks may not be keeping up with inflation.

A small subset of this group consists of the ones who are making it big. They're living a better lifestyle and can be found on golf courses, tennis courts, and other places where they can see and be seen by the power brokers of the community. If they need dentistry, they tend to go to the office that caters to those they're trying to emulate. It's not an easy group to cultivate and it takes considerable time and money to do it.

Next on the age ladder are those with kids in high school and college. I lump these together since getting those offspring an education is an overriding economic factor in most parental lives. These folk are either saving for college tuition or writing checks for it.

Generally speaking, they've about hit their peak earning power. They may be as insecure about their jobs as they were when they were in their twenties. The companies they work for are always looking to transfer part of their operations out of the country to eliminate high wages. Jobs are constantly being eliminated by mergers and buyouts. Many large corporations have also discovered it's cheaper to hire someone younger for that job and put the older worker out to pasture. Or simply fire them.

The resident experts I'm acquainted with feel this trend will continue so long as there's a backward country where wages are low. No company is immune to the siren song of slimming an operation to increase or maintain profit margin without raising prices.

I point out these facts to illustrate a point. You must be something of an economic forecaster in making your selection of a site for your office. What you feel will happen in the reasonably near future will affect your present decisions.

A number of breadwinners in the age group under discussion have stepped out on their own and opened their own businesses in the last couple of years. They're equally insecure, but generally optimistic, about their chances for ultimate success. They are just as dependent on the economy of the area you're looking at as you'll be. Since they've done a lot of research in determining their opportunities, they're a good source of information.

A fair number of the men in this age group, in addition to maintaining a household, are also paying alimony and/or child support. This is a hidden situation that will erode a lot of otherwise disposable income. I might point out that their ex-wives are having a hard time, too. Very few are living in the lap of luxury—contrary to what their ex-husbands might say!

The last group consists of what is usually referred to as the elderly. Once considered the false tooth generation, they've had the benefit of better care early in their lives and are routinely looking at bridges, crowns, partial dentures, and other lucrative treatments. This generation is more health conscious as a class than any other, and will many times scrimp to pay for what they feel they need.

I should point out at this juncture that my definition of "elderly" is a very loose one. When related to our profession, it's a matter of outlook as much as anything else. Loosely translated, "elderly" would mean anyone who's over 55, has his or her children all educated, and is thinking of retiring or has retired. The upper limits of this class extend to the time they either pass on or head for a nursing home. Remember, the same social and economic strata demarcations still apply.

I would caution you not to assume all elderly are merely surviving on a governmental handout. As a whole, this group controls a surprising percentage of individual wealth in this country.

A great number of practitioners make the mistake of treating older patients as either nonpeople or terminal. While seniors do sport an amazing number of infirmities, the vast majority are vital, active people who will flock to any practitioner who treats them like human beings.

That last is an opinion, of course; prejudiced by having made a decent living in a retirement area by catering to the needs and wishes of these patients. It can be a rewarding practice, although it's sometimes discouraging to realize a fair percentage of your patient pool shows up in the obituary column each year.

Do not dismiss serving these patients out of hand. The long held myths about their economic woes are just that. The majority do have money, pay their bills well, and accept treatment more often than their juniors. Their economic fortunes are less tied to the economy of an area than those who work. Their family responsibilities are diminished, making them potentially desirable patients.

A slightly smaller pool of seniors is required to make a living. There is generally less competition for their disposable dollar from your colleagues. You must, however, be willing to deal with some eccentricities and increased demands on your time.

One other small point should be made. The population group you're initially dealing with will change as you—and they—mature. At various times in your professional career, it may well be you'll be dealing primarily with each of these age groups before you reach your own retirement time.

Having considered all these factors and narrowed things down to a town or general neighborhood type within a city, it's now time to pick a more specific office location.

# Chapter 3

# Narrowing Your Selection

Whether you're starting your own practice or buying one, the choice of an ideal location for your office is extremely important. Retail giants, from monster department stores to franchised fast food joints, spend truly big money researching just the right spot. They don't do this without a good reason. If it works for them, it should work for you.

I do not mean to intimate that your life savings and those of your unborn children should be squandered in a research effort that rivals Wal-Mart, but a bit of real investigation is in order. One thing you need to remember is that every town is different. What may be a perfect office site in Kansas City may be less suitable in Atlanta.

Reality dictates you'll have to compromise because of availability of either land or office space for sale or lease. There are just so many square feet vacant next to a bank that's less than three blocks from a medical center, on a well travelled thoroughfare that isn't, at the same time, a congested race track.

What I would like you to remember as you plow onward is you're known by the company you keep. Cozying up between a donut shop and a shoe repair cubbyhole quite possibly isn't the image you may want to project.

On the other hand, if it's the only space available for 10 miles, you may have to compromise if everything else is favorable. At least you'll be aware of what you're getting into and can make appropriate adjustments in marketing plans and soundproofing against racket coming from next door.

If you feel this example is too extreme, you'll have to excuse me. I'm only trying to find the largest basic common denominators I can to give you something to measure by.

For discussion purposes, let's divide practice settings into three subdivisions. Urban, suburban, and rural. Let's start with urban.

## AN URBAN VIEW

An urban office is one located in the heart of a reasonably large community. Any metropolitan area much above 50,000 qualifies for this designation. It can also apply to a smaller community in which there is a central business district and one or more remote, separate shopping areas. This may be the downtown area of a real metropolis, the financial center of the city, or the medical heart of the town, snuggled up against the biggest hospital. It may be a close congregation of businesses, where a large number of office workers or other potential patients are concentrated during working hours.

For the specialist, this is often the best place to locate. The central location usually means you're able to draw from the largest number of referring colleagues who are the life blood of most specialty practices. For the general practitioner, there are some serious drawbacks.

Let's look at the specialist first. As I just noted, with the possible exception of orthodontics, some prosthodontists who advertise, and possibly a well-established periodontist, most specialists depend on their colleagues for a living. While accessibility and convenience are a plus, most patients will put up with a bit of adversity in going to a specialist's office.

For the patient, a visit to one of these exalted personages is an event. It's not looked on by the public as a continuing relationship, even though in some cases it may be more enduring than their association with their family dentist. Traveling an additional distance, hassling with parking or public transportation, and other adversities are most often taken in stride.

There are limits, however. If the accessibility factor is too great, you may eventually find referrals drying up as patients complain to whoever referred them.

Local conditions also play a part in an urban practice. New York, for instance, has an entirely different set of ground rules than, say, Los Angeles. You might be hard pressed to find a truly suburban location on the island of Manhattan. You'd be equally hard pressed to find a similar dominant single central urban setting in Los Angeles. By definition, Los Angeles should be looked on as a collection of closely spaced smaller communities, each with its own central business district. A Californian might consider a New Yorker's neighborhood practice as ultra-urban. The New York dentist might wonder how a Long

*Narrowing Your Selection*

Beach colleague ever manages to have his patients find him in the confusing maze of smaller shopping areas.

Most urban areas fall somewhere in between. For the general practitioner, there are some advantages and big disadvantages to the central urban or traditional downtown location.

First, consider the parking situation and high rent costs in multi-story buildings. Real estate is at a premium in these locations, and the cost is passed on to the renter. Purchasing a practice site is nearly out of the question.

When figuring rental costs in one of these situations, you must also factor in parking for yourself, your employees, and quite possibly for your patients. These costs can mount up rapidly. I recently saw one doctor's parking bill which approached his actual rent.

There's also the problem of visibility. If the only on-site advertising you can have is a discrete sign on your door and a directory or two in the lobby, you become invisible. You must find some other way of getting your name out in front of the public.

The large advantage is a mammoth pool of office toilers within a block or so of your office. They are all potential patients. Maybe. In most cities, they come streaming in every morning and flee back out to the suburbs at night. Their roots are not in the office they take coffee breaks in.

They may change jobs and thus move from your immediate area. Most of those available toilers are in clerical positions. They're often single and have very few roots. What ties they have may be in an outlying area where their families are. They may, quite paradoxically, prefer to take off a full day to go to a dentist near their residence rather than slip off for an hour or so to visit you next door!

If you do feel this is the type of situation that will be most advantageous to you, look closely at the building you're headed for. Have long and serious talks with the building manager or leasing agent about what restrictions there are on additional plumbing, wiring, and partitioning.

Investigate the services furnished. For example, will their normal janitorial people provide adequate service to meet OSHA and other requirements, or will you have to be responsible for this?

In many cities, security in office buildings is a problem that should be carefully investigated and even covered in a lease. If there's a parking garage associated with the building, it should be included as part of the security system. Pay special attention to how gaining entrance is handled after normal business hours.

Visit the building at various times of the day to see what the elevator service is like at peak hours. Check the lobby for cleanliness, loiterers, or strange odors. Look closely at the lobby directory for other medical professionals. If they're there, chances are the building operators understand and are prepared to furnish the specific requirements you may need.

What kind of parking facilities are offered? While a few of the residents of our metropolitan areas do not depend heavily on the private automobile for mobility, most do. A patient will not take kindly to having to walk much more than a block or so to get to your office. The closer the parking garage or lot, the better.

Talk to other tenants about the building's drawbacks. I recall consulting an accountant some years back whose office was in one of the most prestigious edifices in that city. I have no idea who occupied the floor directly overhead, but either they weighed 400 pounds and wore lead boots, or the building was not sufficiently soundproof. Possibly things like that don't bother you, but if I'd been a tenant, I'd have had to take tranquillizers within six months.

The axiom stated earlier applies to all office choices. It's the saw about being known by the company you keep. If you move into a down-at-the-heels building with down-at-the-heels tenants, expect down-at-the-heels patients who will expect down-at-the-heels fees. The rent may be better than in another location, but you'll probably lose more than the difference in your total gross income.

Don't misunderstand. There's nothing wrong with appealing to these less successful people, as long as you know you're doing it and gear your practice accordingly. There's a continuing need for this type of practice, and it can be a rewarding one. Just don't expect to specialize in full-mouth reconstructions when you're setting yourself up to attract minimum-wage patients.

You may do better to locate on the fringe of a central area. In many cities, as the business district expands vertically, professionals flee to the edge of the district. This is especially true in formerly smaller cities that are growing and haven't had time for the surrounding residential areas to become blighted.

But be careful! In cities that are more stable and growing slowly, if at all, these spots may be only a block or so from some of the worst slums in the country. Snoop before you sign a lease. (Snooping will be dealt with directly.)

In the more agreeable areas, enterprising investors have found older houses to refurbish or tear down and replace with small single-use offices. Parking becomes far less of a problem and traffic congestion is less. You're still more or less centrally located, but you have advantages more often associated with a true suburban location.

In these offices, rent is usually somewhat less than right in the middle of things. Plumbing and other remodeling is less of a hassle. You also have the advantage of being able to erect a sign large enough to be read by passers-by. You will, however, probably have to arrange for your own maintenance and janitorial services. That may include taking care of any landscaping, which at times can be a major expense item.

For the specialist, this type of office may provide significant advantages over the true downtown location. For the general practitioner, there are still a lot of negatives.

Unless there's a significant desirable residential population quite nearby, the general practitioner has no ready patient base handy to cater to. He or she must range far afield to glean patients. Even if it's on a fairly well-traveled street, the advertisement factor gained from a sign is negated by the fact everyone is whizzing by on the way to somewhere else. Thus the office site becomes effectively inconvenient for the patient to reach.

For the specialist and sometimes for the general practitioner, a second alternative centralized location may exist. This is a medical building snuggled up next to a major hospital. A building may house as few as a dozen offices or be a multi-storied affair rivaling those glass-and-steel towers downtown. Rents are often steep and sometimes parking is a bit difficult. There is the advantage of sometimes obtaining referrals from physicians next door. Patients tend to view these offices as prestige locations indirectly inferring superior treatment. This can translate into the ability to charge bigger fees and gain greater acceptance for more expensive treatment.

Two bits of caution about hospital-based locations. First, many good hospitals are downsizing. Some are making moves to the suburbs. Some may have quiet plans to close their doors entirely or limit the services they provide. This can adversely affect your available patient pool.

The other caution concerns the cozy arrangements many medical centers are entering into for the purpose of providing managed care. You may find you're almost required to join a provider group you really don't want to associate with. This unforeseen alternative might ultimately involve finding another location within months.

For the general practitioner, this type of location holds more advantages than the true central area, although the drawbacks just mentioned for the specialist also apply. There's something of a potential patient pool from the employees in the building and from the staff at the adjacent hospital—

depending on how close you are to that facility.

One other advantage may be the security offered to the parking lot or garage that services the hospital. This may make it possible to offer alternative hours in cities where this would otherwise be impossible or extremely hazardous.

## SUBURBAN CONSIDERATIONS

For the general practitioner, the mass migration to the suburbs in the last 50 years is a clarion call to follow. Don't forget, though, that some of the older suburban areas have moved from the classification of suburb to that of small metropolitan areas.

This occurs when people living there are not in the least dependent on the parent city. They may go months without ever venturing into the core area that originally spawned their present living space.

It's hard to come up with a good all-encompassing definition of a suburb. It may be a small town that's been engulfed by the onrushing growth of a larger city. It may be a planned, self-contained community laid out by a developer to provide not only bedrooms but complete amenities for people working elsewhere. It may be nothing more than a haphazard collection of individual houses huddled together for protection against the night. It may be so new that the tree twiglets are still tied down to keep them from blowing away. Or it may be old enough to be housing a second or third generation of families. As diverse as this sounds, there are real similarities for the dentist.

First, most suburban areas are comparatively homogenous. By this I mean it basically has attracted people of similar education, income, and cultural values or aspirations. In the newer areas there's a tendency toward age uniformity, too.

The businesses that locate nearby to serve these people know their clientele. They offer valuable clues as to who their customers are. Health clubs, hobby shops, and the like are potential treasure troves of information just as valid as the clothing in the department stores.

Older metropolitan suburbs that were once fair-sized towns on their own often mimic their big brother cities by having a substantial central business district. They may even sport mini-suburbs all their own, all encased within the overall parent metropolitan area. Some of the smaller, older areas may even maintain the air and fiction of a small town, although usually it's just that—a fiction. Others may be beginning to suffer the same rot that's affected the central city they once served as bedrooms for and are now intimately attached to.

Something of a paradox has occurred with these suburbs. As more people moved further away from their city jobs, more businesses opened in once remote neighborhoods to serve them. Big downtown stores spouted branches offering additional employment for the residents. With the advent of the mall, many suburbs became replicas of the city they flank. Eventually core businesses moved to be closer to their work force. This makes it difficult at times to tell whether you're dealing with a suburb or an urban setting when choosing an office. The line is blurred badly in some cities.

More typically, a suburban setting has no real core. Retail business is found either in a mall or in strip shopping centers along major thoroughfares running through or adjacent to the area. Except in the largest, there's little concentration of medical offices to nestle up to. Dental offices tend to be solo or small, partnership practices settled into various neighborhoods within the community. At the present time even the most militant of insurance-backed HMO operations tend to farm out their dental business to these smaller independent operators and groups without playing favorites.

Most dental offices are located in free-standing buildings or in the small strip center shopping areas. Large malls do sometimes have office space available for professionals, but their leasing arrangements and the location reserved for office space is not generally desirable. The mall atmosphere also tends to diminish the professional air most dentists wish to maintain. The negatives make the mall alternative less than totally ideal. Success in this atmosphere takes a very special person with definite talents.

Perhaps a definition or two is in order at this point. So there's no confusion, I'm using the term "mall" to indicate a cluster of stores whose entrances are located on a central area closed to all vehicular traffic. Parking access may be somewhat remote from a desired location. The strip center has similar retail establishments opening onto the parking lot with the only interconnection between shops being the sidewalk or parking lot. The term "shopping center" refers to either, or to any other hybrid collection of businesses.

The strip-center office provides both advantages and disadvantages. The plus side of the ledger includes such items as high visibility, easy parking, fair amounts of traffic directly on the sidewalk in front of the office, comparatively moderate rent, and little or no exterior maintenance.

The disadvantages may be in the neighbors you have. Fast food chains, small taverns, shoe repair shops, and the like create an unprofessional atmosphere you may wish to avoid. Areas which include a bank, specialty shops and possibly another professional or two are the best. The foot traffic by the door more likely includes the type of people you want as patrons.

A warning. In some of these facilities there can be such a thing as too much traffic. Avoid the strip center located on the access road of a freeway or the main artery running through the area. More specifically, I'm referring to one that has all parking directly connected to the highway and where the offices are strung out on the frontage.

Unless you're part of a major collection of businesses of the type you wish to be remembered with, you'll be totally missed in the automotive rush to get from here to there. In some spots of this sort, getting out of and back into the traffic flow is nearly suicidal, creating a negative attitude in the potential patient's mind. You're usually better off in an area that's served by a secondary thoroughfare.

The same holds true for the converted house, single occupancy dedicated office or small grouping of professional offices. The exception is the strip center devoted solely to professionals including other medical types. This can allow you to thrive on a main artery.

A warning. Try and avoid being the only professional in one of the large strip centers unless it's brand new. There's bound to be a reason no one else has located there.

If there's a particular neighborhood within the suburb which appeals to you, try and locate somewhere on the main road that leads into it. Zoning restrictions may hamper your first choice, but do the best you can. When possible, pick a spot that has some visibility so people will quickly know you're there.

Parking in a suburban location is even more critical than it is in a more urban setting. Your patients will paradoxically resent having to walk as much as a half block to get to your door—even if they're planning on a two mile jog the minute they leave!

If you do opt for a neighborhood practice, approach the area as if it were a mini suburb, making the same assessments you would with the larger drawing area. Check the stores and any adjacent houses to see who you'll potentially be dealing with. Pay particular attention to the following chapter which deals with selecting a specific location for your office.

**SMALL TOWN CONSIDERATIONS**

Small towns tend to be the easiest to assess. Everything is right out there for you to see. If there are warts, there's no real way the community can hide them.

Let's define a small town. It's any community or more properly, any trade area which has no, or minimal, medical or dental specialists immediately available, is under 10,000 or so in population, and is an hour's drive from the nearest reasonably metropolitan center offering the specialty treatment just mentioned.

Even here, any definition has to be a bit fuzzy. There are sections of the northeast where one essentially small town is butted right up to the next. There's little or no free open space between. In the southwest, you may find towns as far away as 50 miles from their nearest neighbors and literally hundreds of miles from the nearest city.

The situation where there's a string of small villages along the highway presents something of a conundrum. Some may not have a dentist but have the population to support one or possibly several dentists. Even though the raw statistics are there, any dentist moving in can possibly starve due to a community tradition of going to the next town for all medical needs. In all other respects these places may be quite chauvinistic, but this one area of commerce is unique.

A parallel situation may be found in large residential subdivisions where there is little or no provision made for businesses. These bedroom neighborhoods may have to rely on the a commercial area miles away from the inhabitant's front doors. Barriers to opening an office in locations of this sort may be placed by zoning restrictions which overlay the more insidious ones created by custom.

You, perversely, may find a similar situation working two ways. In this instance the physicians are all congregated in one town and the dentists in another! It doesn't make a great deal of sense, but things like this do occur. Peer at the yellow pages of a few local phone books to get a feel for the prevailing custom before you make your final decision.

In doing your assessment, remember, the more isolated the community, the more resourceful the dentist must be. This is one of the rare instances where professional skills may dictate a location choice for the general practitioner. Those wisdom tooth extractions the urban dentist won't touch under the most extreme circumstances are routine for the remote country practitioner. When referrals mean a two-or-three hour drive with only the vaguest lip service to the speed limit, few patients hold still long for the dentist who cannot handle almost everything that walks in the door.

It's imperative you assess any small town critically. Many of these hamlets are slowly withering away for lack of outside income flowing in. Young people move away in search of a more exciting life. Those remaining are not always the best and brightest progeny. Be sure the small town you pick has a good economic base, preferably one that's growing.

Office location in these small towns is often a matter of taking what's available. There's usually a business district which may or may not be on the highway. In a stable town, someone must retire, die or move away for office space to become available. You may have to rent or buy a house next to the business district in order to find reasonably suitable accommodations.

Small towns are usually less stringent in their zoning and building codes, although you shouldn't count on this. Quite often the laws are on the books, but not enforced. However, if there's a power struggle going on for control of city hall, you may find yourself in the middle of a quagmire of pettiness when you try to get anything official done.

This can be due to a colleague fearing competition from a newer, possibly more up-to-date intruder. The best situations are where there are already at least three or four dentists in the community or where there are none.

In any small town large enough to support you, there'll be a good and bad part of town. You should try your best to locate your office in the narrow neutral zone. This is not usually a problem as most of the other businesses will also be lined up there. If you must make a choice, pick the good side, but try to get as close to that neutral zone as possible.

Where there are two business districts, one on the highway and one on the old main street or square, you may have a choice. Generally speaking, you're just as well off to stay off the highway even if it's only a half block away. In most small towns your arrival will be something of an event and the majority of the inhabitants will know you're there within a week, maybe even hours!

The small town offers a couple of positive aspects to balance the relative professional isolation you'll find. Some of the basic costs will be a bit lower. Rents tend to be slightly less, but don't count on there being a big differential. Construction costs may be greater in a small town than they are in the city.

Wages do tend to be lower, too. While you may have to train an assistant, you'll find they're usually willing to work harder for less than their city counterparts. If you treat them well, they'll probably be more loyal, too. If they're true locals, they can be great practice boosters.

The downside to this is that finding a hygienist may be a luxury you can ill afford, especially at first. If there's one living in your area and there are other dentists, chances are she's already working for them. The psychology of having the same hygienist in two offices in the same town may be a negative for both you and your colleague. Being the new kid on the block, this may work to your disadvantage more than the other dentists.

Since I'm in the business of pointing out realities, I should warn the ladies that they face a bigger battle for full acceptance in a small town than they probably will in a city. Your strong selling point will be the perception that you possess an ability to handle children better than a man.

Chauvinistic? Of course. But perceived facts, no matter how potentially erroneous, are facts that cannot and should not be ignored. You'll eventually be accepted once you prove your full worth, but it's going to take a bit longer and require more diligence than it would for your male counterpart in the same circumstances.

One thing that should be mentioned in this discussion is that the smaller the town you're in, the more visible your personal life. There's an anonymity to big city living that's missing in small towns. In hamlets, everything you do will be under a microscope and subject to criticism and gossip. It can be downright malicious at times!

You may also have to contend with unfounded escalation of an innocent fact. A simple cough or two at the wrong time may grow through wagging tongues into a galloping, even terminal, case of tuberculosis! This exact scenario happened to a colleague of mine. It took several months for him to overcome this falsehood.

Another requisite of small town practice is, you'll be expected to become a real part of the community. This means church, civic, and school matters. If your outlook, lifestyle, and beliefs are out of the mainstream thinking of your projected community, the censure a small town can heap on you means the potential destruction of your practice almost overnight. Be prepared to be square! You'll definitely not have the personal freedom you might expect elsewhere.

You'll note I've left out the advantages of small town living. They are numerous. Things like a slower pace, getting to really know your patients, the true sense of community, and many others are powerful considerations. For the right individual, they far outweigh the often lower net income potential afforded in the bigger community. It's a case of giving up some things to gain others.

Your decision as to where you want to settle down should be part of your early self assessment. Once you've narrowed your choice significantly, it's time to look for the perfect office!

## Chapter 4

# Double Checking Your Choice

Once you've fairly-well settled with a great deal of specificity on a location, there are still a number of things you must do before you commit yourself to anything. The first is to double check your information. The other is to see what your competition is. The latter will be discussed shortly.

There was a brief mention earlier about trends for a state, region, city, hamlet or neighborhood. This applies with double force to the specific site you're honing in on. In that regard you need to ask yourself an extremely important question: How long do I intend to practice in this location?

Many decisions will be simplified by an honest answer and may make other decisions almost automatic. For example, it doesn't matter if urban blight is creeping in on your dream location if you're only planning on staying for a four or five year period. It matters greatly if you're planning on settling in for 20 to 40 years.

It's almost too obvious to point out that if you're openly looking at a five-year stint, you'd be foolish to attempt to buy or build your own facility. You'd also be unwise to spend more than the required minimum in remodeling leased office space. It can also have a bearing on the type of lease you demand.

Sometimes the answer to that question may be dictated by outside forces not under your control. One of those forces is where the city fathers are trying to direct community development. Though it may not be trumpeted, this is a very common occurrence.

How do you discover this direction? It's often surprisingly simple. In most towns, one of the first places you need to go to is the planning commission. This may be local or it may be state, depending on the locality. It doesn't hurt to check both of them. Also, within some states there are regional planning authorities coordinating the pipe dreams of the various local entities within its boundaries.

These planning commissions handle such mundane and arcane things as resource allocation. These include water supply, highway planning and the coordination of governmental construction to accommodate future area growth. The commission may have authority to designate wilderness areas, historical districts, population density limits, environmentally sensitive spots and the like. In a way, they can function as a pre-zoning authority.

You may not think their grandiose manipulations could possibly affect you, the insignificant dentist, but they can. What happens if your great office that's just beginning to pay off is suddenly condemned because of the new expressway? How will you cope when you find you're in the middle of a historic building district that severely restricts your freedom to modernize or remodel what's there? What if you can't take out a tree that's ruining your office's foundation simply because it's on some endangered species list for your area?

True, a real estate agent should be up-to-date about such things. After all, it's their business. Unfortunately, they aren't always as sharp as they should be. Equally true, you may have some recourse in court later to recover damages from someone, but by the time you collect, the settlement may be of value only in stretching your retirement budget.

On occasion, your friendly banker may steer you away from some of these snares. This is especially true if that loan you've negotiated hinges on your continuing practice in the location you've selected. However, pardon the pun, don't bank on it! Banks are notorious for hiring the cheapest help available. Translation, they usually get what they pay for.

To put that in plainer terms, if one of these people warn you away, listen to them. If they assure you everything's fine, double check!

This may not be the perfect place to make the point, but real estate people are in the business of selling and/or leasing real estate, not making you rich. They're being paid by a seller or landlord, not you. They have no real moral obligation to look out for your interests. They have no immediate interest in your financial well-being beyond your having enough cash for the lease or down payment. So, buyer beware!

I've already made the case for putting the practice in a location that has the type of patients you want. It's time to see how to double check your pick.

You need to start at the center of your selected location and travel every street for at least 15 blocks in every direction. While this is crucial in the urban and suburban setting, it isn't a bad idea to try it in the rural location. You'll learn volumes about the place. There are three things you're looking for.

The first is population density. If you're smack dab in the middle of a batch of high rise apartment buildings, there are a lot of bodies available to fix teeth in. That's great. Or is it?

In most of America, apartments mean footloose. Few people rent an apartment and stay there for their entire lives. While turnover rates vary in different parts of the country, in my neck of the forest a two-to-three-year stint is about the limit. It also follows that the more Spartan the accommodations, the higher the turnover rate, to say nothing of the meager disposable income of the denizens.

On the other end of the scale would be the grand stately homes where each takes up a half city block. A great neighborhood to be in, but how many people are actually hidden behind those impressive front doors? Don't ever forget you'll never have them all for your patients.

Most suitable areas for a practice fall somewhere in between. Ask yourself if those people you're spying on are what you want for patients.

You may find in some areas it's a good idea to take the after-dark tour, too. More than one residential area has been known to entirely change character after the sun goes down. Your ideal may turn out to be something other than the warm friendly residential area in post-twilight time. You may accuse me of going to extremes in being cautious, but a quick trip to the nearest police station to inquire about the comparative crime rate surrounding your dream spot might not be amiss.

Please take the time to dig deeply. For example, consider the following question: Are a large number of "For Sale" signs in the front yards of your area a positive or a negative indication of the neighborhood or community's economic health? The surface answer might well be negative. People are trying to get out before a bubble of some sort breaks.

Believe it or not, those same signs may be a result of a tremendous economic expansion! I'll cite my own small hamlet as an example. During the past five years, as much as 20 percent of the homes have been for sale at any given time. Yet the community has nearly doubled in size. Property values have risen dramatically. People are selling their homes and investing the profits in building larger accommodations, sometimes lowering their mortgage payments at the same time! Several formerly underemployed dentists are now adding staff as a direct result of this push. One has recently taken on an associate.

The point? Look deeply into the economic health of your community or neighborhood and don't be fooled by initial appearances.

The second thing you need to look for is the economic status of those people living in the area you covet. You don't need to knock on doors and ask embarrassing questions to get a good feel for this. Look at the size and condition of the houses or apartment buildings as you go by. Note the way the yards are kept. The type, age, and body damage on the cars in the driveways or parked along the curb can be good clues to the overall affluence of the residents.

Even such unmentionable things as garbage will tell you extra bits about the area. No, you don't have to go snooping in the corner dumpster. The mere presence of chronically overflowing dumpsters or garbage sacks or cans that've been out for a couple of days is an indication the city considers this a second class spot.

You'll find a neighborhood on the way down has worse streets than the better neighborhoods. The local appraisal office or possibly your banker will tell you if property values are being reduced for tax purposes. The condition of area parks is instructive. In some urban areas even the noise level is significant!

The third item of concern is the trend the area is taking. Practically all neighborhoods go through a cycle eventually. It begins with new construction of homes as the city grows. Every house then passes through several owners who maintain it, even upgrade it. As the age increases, the upkeep gets to be a continuing escalating process and it's again sold to one of three types of people.

The first type doesn't really care about the appearance of the domicile or whether that shingle is loose over the front porch. They merely want basic shelter from the elements. They don't intend to spend a dime on the place. Even if they were so disposed, they probably don't have the dime to spend.

Type two is the absentee landlord who intends to rent the place for a few years and write the original investment off as rapidly as possible. It may not be a tax dodge, but it comes close. This owner may subdivide a large house into several smaller units, thereby increasing profit. Because the renters aren't the type who have that much pride in their abode, they don't complain, allowing maximum profit from minimal investment.

Type three has a sneaking suspicion if he or she holds onto the property long enough, the land beneath the building will turn a profit on its own merits.

In the meantime anything that can be milked from it will be gravy on the mashed potatoes.

In any case, the decline soon becomes visible to the passer-by. That includes you. Or should.

There's a purpose to highlighting this decline. An area of this sort may be a good place for a dental office—or maybe not. The practice approach must be entirely different than it would be in a more upscale area. This is no place for you if you want to do full-mouth reconstructions!

The next stage is obvious urban decay. No description or explanation of this is necessary, nor do I need to relate it to your chances to make a really good living in such surroundings. The exception is when there's a tremendous patient pool and you're willing to do emergency treatment as your bread and butter. It can be lucrative, but it's hardly a challenge to your professional skills. Approach this type of practice with open eyes and a hard heart. Collections will be difficult at times!

There is an exception to this decay situation when dealing with a small, rural town whose economic base is primarily agricultural. Many of these byways look far worse than they should. In many instances the leading citizenry live in places that would be classified as eyesores in a suburban starter community. The truth is, these people often put their money in their pockets, not their houses. The Joneses just don't give them much to keep up with!

The final stage of change in an area is slum clearance and/or rehabilitation. At this point, those houses which have stoutly withstood all the assaults on their being are cherished as unpolished antique treasures. People who have a longing for hardwood floors and drafty hallways spend many times the original cost of the place to hand sand woodwork and rebuild fireplaces.

It may be this cycle will eventually repeat itself, but so far it hasn't had time in most locales. The refurbishment of neighborhoods is a fairly recent phenomenon. The pertinent thing you need to know is how this cycle will affect your practice when you locate there.

The short answer is, stage one is great. Stage two is questionable, depending on the clientele you wish to attract. Stage three is a disaster for nearly any professional. Making a living under these conditions is chancy at best. Stage four is a bonanza. Your job is to determine which stage your area's in and how far into each part of the cycle it is.

Incidentally, this cycle holds true for apartment houses, commercial properties, and even the most humbly utilitarian of all bits of construction, the disappearing city barn that once held the homeowner's horse and carriage.

## FORECASTING THE FUTURE

The other thing you're after in your prowl is figuring out where your area's heading and how fast. If the edge of your dream neighborhood is beginning to crumble, but the rest is great, make an assessment of the age and income level of the people you'll be dealing with for the next few years.

One way of doing this is to window shop nearby stores. If they feature $100.00 items in the display case, you're better off than if they stick with $1.98 versions of the same article. The condition of the stores themselves often offers a clue. Are they sparkling clean, sporting well-groomed salespersons? Or are they just a step or two above seedy?

I seem to be emphasizing this at every turn, but it bears repeating over and over. Fit your location to the type of practice you'll be comfortable with. Not everyone has the temperament to deal with the movers and shakers of the world. Go where you'll be fulfilled emotionally as well as financially!

For the sake of being thorough, I must invade a very touchy area of today's society. That is the ethnic or cultural component of a neighborhood. This mix is the proverbial two-edged sword that may cut against you or in your favor in your quest for financial success.

An example. Two dentists open an office in an area where the inhabitants are recent immigrants and where English is a distant second language. Obviously, a large percentage of these people have little or no communication skills in English. One of the dentists speaks the imported foreign tongue and the other doesn't. Decide for yourself which has the better chance of garnering the lion's share of the patients.

Similar scenarios may be drawn for any easily identifiable race, creed, or color. Be cognizant that the ideal conception of a bias-free society is not currently realistic. Even if you can trace your family tree back to the Mayflower, you may find your surname is an advantage or disadvantage in any given situation. Factor that information into your final assessment of your choice.

Because this is such a touchy subject, I shall stop, make sure my foot is out of my mouth, and suggest you proceed onward to the next step in your evaluation. That will be determining what your competition might be.

# Chapter 5

# Scoping Out Your Potential Competition

It may sound unprofessional. It may sound sneaky. It may sound unethical. Imagine, going behind a respected colleague's back to see just what he or she's doing. Horrors!

I'd remind anyone whose mind is filled with that kind of idealism that there's something in the world known as making a living. There's nothing in the oath you took forbidding it. You need to know if there's really room for you to prosper. If you're still reluctant, remember that a bad choice may not only hurt you, it may hurt that colleague you're so bent on protecting!

Finding out whether there's space for you involves more than a head count to see if there are enough spare bodies around for you to cater to. It incorporates what type of patients they might be and just how well their needs are being met by the other practitioners already toiling in the area.

A point to ponder. If the opportunity looks so great on first inspection, why hasn't someone else already moved in and tied their caboose onto this local gravy train?

No matter how apparently wide open an area looks, you should know what's going on behind the scenes in your colleagues offices. For instance, I don't think you'd consider opening a farm equipment dealership in the heart of New York City without giving serious thought to your chances of selling a combine or two to the locals.

The fact there's little or no apparent competition should be a warning sign. If there's only one dentist in that town of 20,000, there's a reason. A darned good reason, too. Generally the reason is that inserting any more practitioners into the economy would mean they'd all go broke.

This example, by the way, is real. There's a town on the Mexican border that was in precisely this exact situation a few years ago. The dentist-to-population ration was horrible, something like 1/19,000. Any sane analyst who merely looked at the figures would reason it was a spot that desperately needed more dentists.

So what if the climate stank, the winds blew dust into every cranny and the language barrier was formidable? Rotten teeth know no boundaries of this nature. Kids plus candy equals cavities. The average, or mean, or median, or some other measurement of personal income wasn't all that bad—on paper. Why was the area so under-served?

There was, in fact, a very good reason. The wage scale was absolutely miserable and at the same time unemployment was off the charts. A relatively small number of extremely wealthy people skewed the averages. Practically no one in town could afford a dentist. Those that thought they might if the price was right crossed the border to the sister city on the Mexican side where treatment was offered at a fraction of the U.S. cost. The quality might be suspect, but the price was great!

This economic skew was lost on some distant federal bureaucrats. During the time when Uncle Sam was insistent on mandating everything, there was the prevailing notion on the Potomac that no niche in the country could escape having uniform access to health care equivalent to some statistical national average. Every governmental agency that had anything to do with health was desperately trying to get more dentists located in this blatantly blighted community. They heavily subsidized two or three recent graduates as an inducement to settle in this dubious paradise.

The result was predictable. As soon as the federal loot stopped flowing, the dentists started fleeing. There just wasn't enough business to keep them afloat on their own. The few established dentists barely managed to ride out the storm. I feel sure they could've told the social planners what would happen, but no one bothered to ask. Or if they did, they didn't believe the answers.

Which leads obliquely into a warning that your colleagues don't always tell the truth. I assure you, if you ask the preponderance of dentists within a given territory if they need more dentists located next to them, they'll say no. Interview 10 or 100, you'll get a less than optimistic assessment of your chance of success. There's an obvious question here. Are they honestly mistaking the economic signs or are they just trying to hog the whole pie for themselves?

It may be a little of both. In any service-oriented business there are some people who are more successful than others. The less successful ones are probably the honest ones, at least from their perspective. The most successful want to stay as busy as they are. Diluting their patient pool with your presence is not a good way to do that! You therefore need a more objective back-door way of counting the beans they really have and potentially left over for you.

After pooh-poohing statistics earlier, it's time to retrench. There are special situations where number crunching is helpful. For example, one is the rural area with a reasonably limited population that can be accurately counted.

This is probably the one place where you can equate with some reasonable accuracy the dentist/population ratio, the economic base, the unemployment rate, the education level, the prevailing wage scale, and those other measurable items that go into that subtle end product known as potential practice viability.

Statistics won't guarantee success or failure, however. A good part of that is not quantifiable. It involves those imponderables like personality, community acceptance, the way your spouse plays bridge and only the good Lord knows what else. Still, when factored in with other pieces of the puzzle, these numbers can be helpful. Just keep them in perspective and remember the border town just described.

The larger the community, the less the figures apply—unless you can find a totally homogenous, sharply defined population to work with. There may be a "company" town somewhere that fits this narrow description. Otherwise, you need different tools to measure your chances of successfully competing with the other dentists already established.

There are several tricks you can employ to find out how busy those other guys really are. Here are a couple that are relatively simple.

The first is counting the number of employees each existing dental office has. The office with five employees is seeing more patients than the one with only one employee. It's perfectly permissible to hang around and count heads as they arrive in the morning or dash out at night. If the office has more than one dentist in residence at any one time, make allowances for increased efficiency when analyzing your observations.

You can count the number and assay the type of patients going in the door on any given day. Time consuming, but reasonably effective in many cases. If they're all driving shiny new luxury cars, you have a fair idea of the type of practice without ever stepping foot inside. Correlating this figure with the number of employees may give you a good handle on what the practice produces.

If you're really into snooping, keep track of how long each patient is there. If nobody stays more than 15 minutes or so, it's a good bet not a heck of a lot of multiple-unit fixed bridges are being done. Conversely if each patient is incarcerated for a couple of hours, you can be assured they're not just getting their teeth cleaned. (The exception is where there are large numbers of patients and long waiting periods for each. This means inefficiency within. Unless the practitioner refuses to operate out of an appointment book and is downright fantastic, there are dissatisfied patients galore resenting the unnecessary inconvenience.)

How do you assess the information? Here's an example. If 50 or 60 patients flow through the door each day, you're dealing with a true volume practice, one that probably charges low to moderate fees and caters to a particular crowd. Again, the patients' ages, the way they're dressed, and the types of cars they drive will give you valuable clues to the practice thrust. Since you presumably know what part of the patient pool you're after, you may be able to see how filled your particular niche is.

Another sneaky way of peeking at the schedules of other dentists is to call and make an appointment with each of your biggest potential competitors. It's easy. Make up a minor non-emergency that is normally put off by a receptionist until the next available opening in the appointment book. If you announce your availability (provided you have a minimal bit of notice), you may find out how far appointments are backed up.

To be honest, this sneak attack has some built in handicaps. You may call the target office just after someone else has cancelled. Alternatively, the receptionist may have strict instructions to stall and stack patients to give the office the appearance of being busy. A little ingenuity over the phone about the suitability of the proffered time may be enlightening as to the true situation. You can also correlate your information with what you saw in the parking area.

Playing the appointment tag game with the target receptionist may result in offers of a number of appointments. If they're all over the calendar, it indicates an appointment book riddled with holes and a practice that's not going full blast. Getting the same response from the majority of doctors in the target area is not a particularly good sign.

An aside—the artificial delaying and/or stack-scheduling is an ancient trick that's been utilized for decades. The theory is that when people think you're popular and busy, they'll fight to get in your door. There's some validity to the notion, but that's not germane to this book. It merely illustrates the earlier point that you shouldn't give undue weight to any single fact you may gather.

Still another way to assess something of what goes on in the professional community is to find out if there are any practices for sale. Perhaps it's not at all ethical to ride someone else's coattails, but the prospectus put out by practice brokers does contain a limited amount of information about both the immediate area and the dental climate in addition to particulars concerning the practice involved.

View some of this glowing rhetoric with suspicion, since the broker wants to sell a practice at the best possible price. One of the selling points is the viability of the community from which the practice draws patients. If there are several practices for sale in a fairly small radius, there may be a problem looming on the horizon. That bodes ill for the long term. Investigate further if you run into this situation. It may only be coincidence, but wariness is warranted.

You may relax somewhat if the sellers are all of a legitimate retirement age and state that as a reason for the sale. However, if several are offerings of younger dentists with flat incomes who say they want to specialize, be on guard. This new specialization may be to narrow their field of endeavor in better paying patients!

One traditional source which may still be of some value in assessing your colleagues is the supply salesman who services the area you're interested in. If you remember they're in the serious business of selling things to you, you may get a decent amount of information about your future colleagues and the people they serve.

Since the role of the full service supply house has changed drastically in the last 20 years or so, the information may not be as good as it once was. It's difficult nowadays for the salesman to keep as close an eye on the doctors he or she visits as previously. Still, it's worth the time it takes to check.

You may find it helpful to do a bit of investigating about the demographics of the other dentists themselves. If they're all about due for retirement, your youth may appeal to a larger number of patients not otherwise readily available to you.

Check the opportunities for establishing satellite offices. This is extra important if you're a specialist, as this has been a good way to augment income and obtain referrals from one or more remote small towns. (It can be carried to extremes, though.)

You may find it a bit discouraging to learn all the others in your specialty are out three days a week visiting all the hamlets in the vicinity. This could be an indication your dream location is overloaded and your buddies are riding the circuit in order to eke a living.

Additional sources of information on your potential competition are employment agencies that specialize in ancillary personnel for professional offices, recently retired assistants, and hygienists who work in several different offices. It may take a bit of doing to locate the latter two categories, but sometimes it's well worth the effort. They've seen practices from the inside and can provide mountains of information if they're so inclined.

For the specialist, these sources may also provide insights into how satisfied the referring doctors may be with how their patients are being treated by your potential competition. You may indeed find that even though your area is nominally full, a different approach that overcomes the common general practitioner's latent or active dissatisfactions may yield a gold mine.

Which brings us to the final point. Do not rely solely on the surface information you may glean when checking out your colleagues. Use common sense in evaluating it in perspective. It's only one piece in your puzzle. Put everything together before you decide!

# Chapter 6

# Buy, Build Or Lease?

We'll delve into the basic mysteries of each of these options directly, but before that occurs you must decide which is the route you want to take. That is, if you have a choice. At this stage of your deliberations, your money supply may be the deciding factor. Keep that limitation tucked away for ready reference as we proceed.

The other big limiting factor is availability of suitable spots. Some areas don't have an inch of space to rent, but vacant lots or existing structures you can remodel may be plentiful. Other times the reverse is true. For example, the possibility of finding a building for sale in your price range in the middle of an urban location is extremely negligible. Local conditions may make the choice for you.

Whichever way you go, there are basic things to consider. Let's start with an analysis of the merits of each way of obtaining space in which to set up shop. A general discussion of the relative advantages of owning your own place versus the desirability of leasing is in order. There are things good and bad about both. First, let's look at the comparison from the standpoint of leasing.

## LEASING

Leasing (or renting) can be good or bad. On the plus side, it gives you maximum flexibility to correct any mistake you make in your choice of locations. It allows you to upgrade your spot in the community if that becomes advisable. You have less insurance to buy and your maintenance cost is generally less. Your initial out-of-pocket start-up investment is often smaller, a major concern for most dentists embarking on their first practices.

You're spared a portion of the agony and expense you might face with continuing changes in building codes and regulations from all sorts of governmental agencies regarding the building you're in. An example might be the difficulties many property owners had in conforming to the Americans with Disabilities Act.

There's a time factor in favor of renting. Rome wasn't built in a day. Neither is a dental office. In some bureaucratic-bound cities it may take a year or more just to get the permits to erect a simple one-dentist office. A remodelling permit to change the interior of an existing structure is usually obtainable in a matter of days or weeks.

If you move into a mall, strip center, or decent-sized office building, the owners often provide at least partial janitorial service. Even if they only provide cleanup for the exterior of the building, common areas, and parking or landscaping areas, it's one less responsibility you'll have.

There are trade-offs. You may be severely restricted as to the number, size, and character of any advertising signs you may want to place. Your rent can go up dramatically in a very short time if you have the usual commercial lease. That great up-scale dress shop that drew to your very doorway the cream of the potential patients you wanted may suddenly go out of business, to be replaced by a teen-infested pizza hole that doubles as a permanent hostel for roving cockroaches.

You're also stuck with the space available. There may be too much or too little. While I once saw a three-operatory office with all the trimmings tucked into less than 600 square feet, it was extremely cozy. Paying for room to expand may be galling and fiscally grating for the beginner. Failure to provide for expansion in a couple of years may be equally unwise.

Your landlord may also have problems providing the plumbing and electrical requirements of a dental office. Some older office buildings are not easily rewired or replumbed for your needs. Completely soundproofing things like air compressors and central vacuums can be difficult in a limited space. Trash disposal of medical waste may be cumbersome. In larger buildings, your control over the heat and air conditioning is often minimal. This is especially true in structures that have separate units for the two conveniences.

Another hazard may be that of your understanding and cooperative landlord suddenly selling out to someone else. When this happens, all the rules of the game may change overnight unless the lease is extremely comprehensive and most aren't that detailed. There may be new restrictive requirements on the tenants, or the desirable restrictions that were in place may disappear, leaving you awash in a veritable waving sea of flapping plastic flags or blaring loudspeakers hawking a daily special of some sort. You may have to park two blocks away to make room for someone else's customers. The dumpster may be moved right in front of your door.

When your lease is up, you may have to move and leave behind a sizeable investment in remodeling costs. You need an absolute minimum of five years to recoup this investment. Some practices will take longer to make the investment in someone else's property worthwhile.

Worst of all, your landlord may re-lease the space as a dental office. You then find your patients are going there instead of following you a mile down the street.

## OWNING YOUR SPACE

Owning your own office has its good and bad points just as well. The financial ones are a big consideration. On the plus side, your costs are comparatively stable. True, you have the possibility of rising taxes and insurance to contend with, but those are routinely passed on to you in most lease arrangements. Even if they aren't specified, they're hidden in those annual renewal increases most landlords insist on.

When you lease, you're usually stuck with a large initial outlay for outfitting an empty space as a dental office. Assuming you borrow the funds, you'll be required to repay your note over a short period of time, hardly ever longer than the length of the lease. Obtaining a loan for this purpose is often difficult unless you have a long and favorable track record to show a banker, because the bank has little or nothing to repossess if you default. If you own the premises, they have something they can get their mitts on.

When you own an existing building, you may be able to amortize remodeling costs over a longer period, and in all probability, include these as part of your total mortgage package. If you build, nearly all these costs are automatically part of the initial investment, and a much smaller cash outlay is required during those first, leaner years.

Unless you're stuck with a floating mortgage rate, you know from year to year about what to budget for this part of your overhead. At the end of your mortgage period you don't have any payments to make, effectively putting more of your hard-earned money in your pocket. At the end of your career, you have something to sell or rent to provide extra income. This generally beats a pile of cancelled rent checks to burn in the fireplace for a few moments of winter warmth.

There are definite tax advantages, too—at least there were when this was being written. Commercial property is a favorite toy of Congress and advantageous tax treatment shouldn't be considered cast in bronze. Some dentists find it worthwhile to incorporate and lease the building from themselves. Others sell their building to their retirement fund.

Warning! In these murky financial whirlpools, you need the services of both a good accountant and a sharp attorney to steer you away from trouble. With their help, you may learn creative, but legal, ways to utilize ownership of your facility for dual financial purposes.

Besides the monetary aspect, there's a great deal more flexibility in having an office you can expand if need be. If the building is designed carefully, an addition may be possible without too much practice interruption. If the practice grows the way you've planned, there may be a potential for taking in an associate or partner down the line.

There's more freedom in hanging out your shingle—even if it's blinking neon. You can go wild at Christmas without having to fit into someone else's idea of what's appropriate. You may be extremely creative in the exterior treatment of your facility. A children's specialist could even turn the office facade into a mock zoo or carnival.

There are creative alternative ways to put you into your own facility. Here are two examples.

In the first alternative, owning a free-standing building is not the only possibility. There's always the "condo" and "co-op" concepts. In the former, you own your own space, but share common areas such as sidewalks, hallways, parking facilities and the like with the other tenants. Financing may be easier in some instances, especially if a developer is making the sale.

In the co-op, banding together with other professionals to build or buy a building can be a very good arrangement. If your own financial situation is marginal for making a purchase on your own, the buying power of your partners may well outweigh your own problems.

The second common way to get into your own spot is the lease-purchase agreement. Here, you lease your desired building with an option to buy. Some landlords will even offer to carry the mortgage or make part of your lease payment apply to your down payment.

The advantage to such an arrangement is that you have the opportunity to really see your projected area from the inside long enough to make assessments otherwise impossible. You may end up making a somewhat larger lease payment than you might otherwise, but often it can be worth it.

The drawback to this arrangement is your initial investment in leasehold improvements. If you decide not to buy, you will have to chalk up a fair amount of change to experience. If you've agreed to a larger-than-normal lease payment as an inducement to obtain this type of deal, you're out more than you would've been with a straight lease.

Owning does have disadvantages. We've touched on some of them already, but here are a number of others.

You have more obligations and responsibilities. There's maintenance—lots and lots of maintenance. Parking lot paving needs attention often. If there's grass, it requires mowing. Shrubs need trimming. Paper blows in and must be picked up. Roofs need to have that loose shingle attended to. Plumbing stops up. Faucets drip. You're responsible for washing that window, having the floors polished and swept, snow shovelled or plowed, and cobwebs and hornets in your doorway attacked. All sorts of little annoyances seem to crop up weekly. The longer you're there, the more you'll have to do to keep everything ship-shape.

As with the lessee, you have little or no control over what your neighbors do with their property. Most commercial zoning is fairly permissive, which means the climate can change rather rapidly around you. There's no guarantee your property value won't go down the tubes when things deteriorate around you.

I won't bore you with horror stories about condemnation proceedings, road closures in front of dental offices for freeway construction, or snow plows clearing your street and in doing so totally blocking your driveway. Those things can happen whether you rent or own. The difference is, when you own, it's your baby to fix or put up with. You can't just pick up and travel on at the end of the month.

Perhaps the biggest drawback to ownership is that you're stuck. Your margin of error in site selection is slightly above zero. You're in for the long haul. Rapidly changing conditions in the neighborhood may make your formerly desirable location unacceptable to the health of both your practice and your bank account. If you have a good part of your savings invested in that building, you may have financial pains in selling it and moving out in an orderly fashion. You could be in for significant fiscal trauma.

As a general consideration, I would suggest if you're moving to a new area you're not totally familiar with, rent for a while. No matter how carefully you investigate, each location has subtle overtones that will ultimately affect your practice. You're better off initially with that extra flexibility leasing offers.

You may not think so, but this can be true for that old home town of yours. You've probably been away for several years while in school, and maybe more while getting your feet wet in someone else's office.

Though I hate to admit it, I recall being absolutely lost in my own home town after an absence of a scant eight years! The pasture where I'd flown kites was now a monstrous mall surrounded by unfathomable winding strange subdivision streets.

## A SPECIAL SITUATION

There's one exception to the obvious drawbacks of ownership. That's the true small town practice. In a stable or slowly growing hamlet, ownership may be far more advantageous. Often rental property is hard or downright impossible to come by and those businesses near you are generally pretty stable.

If there's a fairly new aggressively managed hospital or similar facility next door to your projected location, you're reasonably safe in investing in property.

Be cautious, however, about cozying up to one of the local physician's offices if there are only a handful of M.D.'s in town. Some communities have developed into armed camps over which physician is better. Planting your flag in the yard of one side will alienate the other immediately. If you find hostilities are present, head for neutral territory.

If you do purchase in a growing small town, take a look at where the growth is occurring and plant yourself as close to it as possible. The chances your property will hold or increase it's value are greater.

In that regard, there's a small secret you should be aware of. Communities of all sizes tend to grow to the north and west unless, or until, there's a natural barrier in that direction. A steep hill or a river are examples. Only then will significant growth proceed in another direction.

Eventually, distance from the commercial center of town also becomes a barrier, allowing growth in another direction. However, when that alternate growth reaches a point of inconvenience, growth will return to the northwest if it's at all possible.

The point? If you're buying property for the long haul, take this into consideration. It can also be a potent factor in assessing where to rent if all other conditions are equal.

While nothing in this chapter should be considered as a dictum for your choice, try to remember the main points when you go out shopping for office space. You may save yourself a headache or two.

# Chapter 7

# Nailing Down
# The Ideal Office

This will be a nuts-and-bolts chapter on finally picking and negotiating for your dream office. Since perfection doesn't exist, there are compromises you'll have to make. The following is intended to make the whole process a little more orderly.

In finding that nearly perfect office, there are space requirements. I mentioned earlier I'd seen a fully functional three-chair office with lab, storage, darkroom, and private office in something less than 600 square feet. I wouldn't recommend it for someone with claustrophobia or five assistants, but the occupant was moderately successful and happy. He'd foregone commodious quarters for the sake of having a remarkably prestigious address. It worked for him for years.

I re-quote that example to illustrate there's no ideal office size. Two of the most contented dentists I've ever met had quarters so different it was hard to think of both offices serving the same function!

One operated in slightly more than 200 square feet. There was one operatory, a minuscule waiting room, and a fair size closet for records. He'd added this cubbyhole to his home. The only drawback he admitted to was when a patient required a bathroom. He'd have to escort them through a connecting door past his own bedroom to the master bath. I still suspect this had something to do with his wife's eventual departure!

On the opposite end of the scale was a veritable palace of more than 3,000 square feet. The waiting room was spacious. There were four operatories, a consultation room, business office, private office, staff lounge, darkroom, sterilizing room, a fully-equipped lab, an equipment room, a room for the panoramic X-ray and three bathrooms—one for patients, one for staff, and one for the doctor. Only the patients' rest room had no shower.

It seems almost incredible, but this very successful doctor was about to expand. She was planning to add two or three additional operatories and another private office with an adjoining bath so she could add an associate! Negotiations were under way for an additional 1,200 square feet!

Presumably your dream quarters will fall somewhere in between. Here the tug of war begins. You have grand plans, but unless a very rich uncle recently died, a limited budget. Now is when you face reality.

Let's agree on basics first. There are five generally accepted basic components required for any dental office. They are: a waiting room, an operatory, a business office, an equipment room, and a rest room. If necessary, the last two may be combined, but it's annoying to have air compressors, vacuum pumps, water heaters, and other such utilitarian necessities where the patients may see, or meddle, with them.

The size of each of these areas is determined by what you're going to put in. Probably, the most critical is the operatory. Different equipment has different space requirements. For example, the arm on an X-ray machine will only extend so far. Cabinetry, sinks, and like items take up a surprising amount of room. So do a unit and chair. You and your assistant need room to maneuver around without constantly banging shins and elbows. Ideally you need sufficient room to maneuver a wheelchair into position to transfer a patient. It's also desirable to have a spot out of the way for that friend or relative who comes to provide an anxious patient with moral support.

Your first trip, therefore, should be to the supply house to learn the dimensions and requirements for all the equipment you have in mind. A bit of advice. You can save money by ordering minor equipment through the mail, but when it comes to major items, this may be false economy. In both the short and long term there are two obvious drawbacks.

I do not mean this as a put-down of the mail order dental supply establishments. The major ones are reputable, honest and generally reliable. The difficulty is they may be several thousand miles away. Realistically, you're completely responsible for the installation of your equipment. The mail people may arrange for an independent technician to install your purchases, but if installation is not completely standard, owing to construction factors in your building, you're the one to solve the problem. The full-service supply house will usually take this burden on itself.

Guarantees may be harder to enforce. If a vital part has somehow been omitted by the factory, you may be frustrated in receiving a prompt replacement. I promise, you're going to be frustrated and overwrought enough dealing with the opening of your office as is. There's no use adding to your blood pressure level and ulcer activity by having to drop everything else to coordinate and oversee independent installers.

As a further pitch for the full-service supplier, many will offer design advice. A few will even draw your basic floor plan for you, including those special wiring and plumbing needs you may not be aware of.

Later, if you wish to save money when replacing old equipment, by all means do so. But, for your first office at least, get all the local help you can.

Having made that point, let's look at some of the other things you need to be aware of, starting with the waiting room.

Yes, it's a waiting room. You may call it a reception area or a patient relaxation lounge, or some other euphemism, but it's still where patients wait. They need a place to sit while they're waiting, and it's up to you to provide as much comfort as possible.

The minimum seating requirement for any reasonably busy dental office is five. Anything less doesn't seem to work well. How much more you provide depends on the type of practice you're planning. My own rule for determining how many bodies you're liable to park at any one time works something like this: For every patient you plan on seeing each hour, you need at least two spots for placing posteriors. If you think you'll be taking care of six patients an hour, that means 12 chairs. It doesn't hurt to add one or two extra over this figure, just in case.

Why the patients-per-hour figure? There are several reasons. The first is there's no guarantee you're not going to get behind and run late. The second is, patients do come early, sometimes as much as a half hour. The third is, patients bring other people with them. Putting your best foot forward demands a place for them to sit. Who knows? They might just end up making an appointment for themselves.

Another phenomenon that should be considered. People don't like to sit jammed up next to strangers. Walk into any professional office where the waiting room is half full and you'll find the people will be spread out as much as possible. For that reason, groupings of two or three chairs are advantageous.

Sofas are great for breaking up that sterile impersonal look most offices have. If you're trying to make your patients feel at ease, the closer you can duplicate a living room atmosphere, the better. However, you'll almost never find more than two people on a sofa at any one time no matter how many it will potentially hold. For that reason, think love seats.

Business offices need enough room to hold records; a receptionist; the normal office equipment like computers, copiers, fax machines and phones; plus enough counter space for someone to work comfortably. A modest amount of storage space is necessary for supplies like insurance forms, stationery, patient questionnaires, and file folders. This stuff takes up a bit more room than you probably realize, so be as generous as you can in your estimate. It's not unreasonable to allow an absolute minimum of 80 square feet for this vital area.

Other rooms can be as small as a broom closet or as large as a skating rink. What other facilities you provide above the basic five is up to you, your dreams, and your pocketbook.

I would offer one small suggestion. You'll need a hall to get from one place to the next. The average residential hall is a nominal four feet wide. That ends up somewhere in the neighborhood of three-and-a-half feet of space to maneuver. If there's going to be more than minimal traffic on this office highway, make it a tad wider if you can. Some of your patients may be overweight, or, perish the thought, you or one of your aides may have celebrated Christmas too generously too many times. Leave enough room for everyone in the office to take a deep breath when passing each other.

A warning. When calculating space requirements and configuration, don't forget to include the space partitioning takes! That drawing indicating your projected operatory would be eight feet wide may actually end up only slightly over seven feet. Depending on what you've opted for, this could be too small to cram your equipment in.

Another warning. The square footage you're interested in may not be suitable for partitioning the way you want. Certain widths do not lend themselves easily to adaptation to the room sizes you're after. This can result in a great amount of wasted or unusable space when you start doing your remodeling. You might find a slightly smaller, differently shaped space will actually accommodate your requirements better.

Once you have some general minimum and maximum requirements in your head, it's time to go shopping for specific space. You may or may not face an immediate problem. Depending on the economic forces at work in the area, you may have plenty of choices—or precious few. As an example I would cite a large city near where I live. Five years ago commercial property was for sale or lease in all sections of the city. The rates and conditions offered were fantastic for the renter and buyer alike. Fully 30 percent of the commercial property zoned favorably for dental offices was vacant.

Today, that same city has a vacancy rate of less than 5 percent. Landlords are raising rents right and left—and demanding far more from prospective tenants. Little or no new construction has been completed to ease the shortage. The best estimates indicate it will take at least 18 months for the pendulum to swing far enough back to allow a decent balance between demand and supply.

This indicates a good, growing economy for the new dentist who picks this town, but he or she will have considerable difficulty in finding a suitable place to operate. Be prepared to do a significant amount of compromising if you're walking into such a situation.

Whatever the local conditions, you'll need some help in locating prime office space. Let's tackle the subject of leasing first. For convenience, the terms "renting" and "leasing" may be used interchangeably.

There are three basic ways to find a place to lease. The first and most obvious is the real estate agent who deals in commercial rental property.

A lot of people have the mistaken notion that when they visit a real estate office, the person they deal with is working for them. This is seldom the case. Unless you're paying them directly, they're working for the other side. Certainly, if they don't sell you on something they have in their inventory, they don't make any money. But it's the landlord that's paying them, not you!

The reason I stress this is, many agents will do their best to steer you to a particular site. They may well have a good financial reason for doing so. Either the particular property they're touting is part of their personal inventory, a company listing, or there's a bonus involved in unloading it.

While there's a fairly standard commission in any given area for handling a rental, if it's been listed by another agent or firm, the commission on the transaction must be split several ways. These folks are understandably out to make a living and should be applauded for their efforts. Just be aware where their money comes from and keep your guard up. These good folks are far more interested in making sure their wallets are full than in making sure you'll be in a spot that is most profitable.

It therefore makes sense to take the time to visit, or at least call, every real estate office serving the area you want. Not all rental property is placed in the multiple listing arrangement between competing offices.

A second source of information is the newspaper. Advertisements offer two separate possibilities for investigation. The first is the want ad section. The second is the financial page.

For variety's sake, let's dispose of the latter in a hurry. Most generally, these ads will be display announcements of varying size and most often pertain to larger commercial properties. Once in a while, though, office buildings will use this route to attract prospective renters. Though it's comparatively rare, you may find just what you're after.

The better bet is the "For Rent, Commercial" section. Some of these properties are offered by real estate brokers and others by individuals looking to save the few bucks commission a professional will charge. If you're not already familiar with the specific building, you should take a quick cruise by and see if it might fit your needs. Or, you can call and get the general information as to size, availability, and tentative rent before you look. Either way, critically examine the exterior presence before you bother wasting time on the inside.

The third way to find something is to tour the area you've decided on and look for "For Rent" signs. Use caution. Your prospective landlord may be a very cheap individual who pinches pennies by avoiding even the newspaper ad, or it may be the building's been vacant for a long time. Either way, there may be trouble for you if you rent it.

An exception is the sign placed by a real estate company. Their advertising budget may not include even the small cost of a classified ad, since handling small rental property isn't a great money maker. Sometimes the phone number listed is that of an agent trying to be sneaky.

Either way, don't be surprised if you get an answering machine. This is just a quick and easy way of screening prospective renters. Both owners and real estate people do this routinely in some areas.

On occasion, you may see a "For Lease, Will Build to Suit Tenant" sign on an empty lot. A version of this may be found on construction sites at strip centers or malls. This option may appeal to you in that you can get precisely what you want in the way of space, plumbing, wiring, and partitioning without laying down a good chunk of your available capital for improvements.

Approach this option with care. You'll pay dearly for the privilege. The cost will be amortized over the period of the lease, along with a good return on the owner's or investor's money. You may be required to sign a longer term, more restrictive lease than you feel comfortable with.

This is nevertheless a viable consideration when checking property. Being able to utilize existing or custom partitions and plumbing is a real money saver. The less remodeling you have to do, the easier and faster it is to get to work to pay for what you do have to alter.

A caution here. Most cities have different building codes for residential and commercial property. These may be confusing and may be in conflict with each other. Many of us have at least a vague notion of what's required in the houses we occupy. Offices are an entirely different world.

An example. The rules about electrical and plumbing minimum standards are usually more stringent for commercial applications. Some communities may even have requirements about such odd things as the thickness of plaster on the walls! If you happen to be renting a structure that was only recently zoned commercial, be sure and check to see how much additional change must be made in order to meet the current codes before plunking down a deposit.

You should have your own plumber, electrician, and/or contractor check the building to see how much trouble there's going to be getting additional wiring and plumbing installed. Having to take a jack hammer to 30 or 40 feet of concrete slab to install a drain isn't fun. Neither is tearing out the ceiling in a couple of rooms to run an electrical supply to your X-ray. You'll be downright devastated if you find you have to replace every bit of wiring because what's already in place isn't run through conduit!

Once you're satisfied you've found what you want, it's lease time. Depending on the real estate market, you may or may not be able to negotiate the rent below what's being asked. Though it may not work, it's worth a try to talk your potential landlord into making concessions on the rent both while you're remodeling and possibly during the first few months while you're getting settled in.

If you're adding to the basic worth of the building, you might ask him or her to pay for part of the upgrading you're doing. If the space has been vacant for some time, such concessions are not unheard of. Don't count on them, though.

Here are a few of the other basic things you should have spelled out in your lease. You may wish to add others, depending on your particular situation, but even the simplest of documents should have the following:

1. The length of the lease and how it is to be renewed. Renewal should be at your option.

2. How any increases (or decreases) in the rent are to be figured when the lease is renewed, or if the lease is for a number of years, how often a change will be allowed, and for what reason.

3. An escape clause. If your landlord doesn't live up to the terms of the lease, you should be able to terminate it without penalty. Try to avoid the customary "disaster" provision the landlord usually tags onto the lease. This gem allows the landlord a number of months to repair or rebuild the premises in case it becomes untenable. You could be in limbo for months!

4. Who's responsible for maintenance on the exterior of the building? If there's landscaping, do you keep it up? Can you maintain it and charge it to the landlord?

5. Who's responsible for plumbing, heating and cooling, gas, etc.? Are you agreeing to maintain ancient improvements that were there before you were born?

6. Does your lease take precedence over other claims on the property?

7. Can you sublet or transfer the lease if you can't continue to practice?

8. How much insurance will both of you be required to carry to protect each other?

9. Is there an arbitration method spelled out for solving any disagreement you and the landlord may have?

10. If the property is condemned for any reason, what damages are you entitled to?

11. What grace period and late penalties are provided for regarding rent payment?

12. Can you cancel the lease if unsuitable neighbors move in next door even if it isn't the landlord's fault?

13. If future changes in zoning, restrictions, or accessibility are imposed on you, what is the landlord's responsibility to take care of them?

14. How much parking space will the landlord guarantee?

15. Will advertising space be provided? What will be the restrictions?

16. In an office building, what will be the access restrictions after normal hours?

17. How many of the improvements you make to the building can you remove at the end of the lease? For example, sinks, or built-in cabinets.

18. In a mall or strip center, will you be required to take part in special promotions or maintain odd hours? What penalties may be imposed if you don't go along?

19. In a mall or strip center, can you veto another dentist coming in and competing with you?

I hope you see the need for an attorney! Nevertheless, don't expect your lawyer to do it all. Unless he or she also practiced dentistry at some time, the chances are he or she won't know all the possible hazards you might face. Be well informed and take an active part in forming the instrument.

One talking point that often does create a concession of some sort is reminding the landlord that professional people are pretty stable renters. Professionals are not usually particularly hard on a building and, for the most part, have a vested interest in seeing the property is well maintained. Not having to constantly go through the hassle of re-renting the place and the prospect of getting it back in good condition at the end of a number of years may be worth a lot to an owner.

Once you come to general terms about the rent and the length of the lease, the next order of business is the lease itself. Don't sign! You may want the place desperately, but back off. Your signature makes you obligated for every clause in that document and you'd better understand *completely* what you're signing. Don't be conned by the common phrase: "It's just a standard lease." No matter how pre-printed it is, there's no such animal. You may think it says one thing, but the legal jargon may actually mean something entirely different.

That document may be typical, but are there things in there you don't want? Most commercial leases I've seen require you to leave all improvements you've made to the building. This can, under some circumstances, include the expensive cabinetry that's essential to your practice. Just because you hung it on the wall shouldn't automatically make it his, but that can happen. What you think you know may not apply. For this and other reasons, *hire a lawyer.*

That's right. I'm sounding like a broken record, and with good reason. No matter how standard that piece of blue-bound paper is, have the expert explain it to you. *Really* explain it to you. You're an expert on teeth, not the law. Leases are generally written for the protection of the landlord and his or her property.

About all you're protected from is premature eviction if you keep your nose clean and pay your rent on time. You may find buried on page 15 an eviction clause written in lawyer jargon that partially negates even that small right.

One important point about leases. Even if you and the landlord are both acting in complete good faith, have it all in writing. Don't make any side agreements, no matter how trivial, that aren't spelled out. The property may change hands. All the new owner will be bound by is what's in black and white. Profit from a very expensive mistake I made!

In this regard, make absolutely sure what your rights are in connection with renewing the lease when it expires. Be certain if you and the landlord do have a disagreement and can't come to terms, you have a reasonable amount of time to decamp. I assure you from that acutely painful personal experience of mine that even a panic move requires a number of months. Vacating in 30 days will force a severe disruption of your practice. If you doubt me, give me a call. I'm still smarting.

The actual negotiating may be done face-to-face, over the phone, through a leasing agent or property manager, by mail, maybe even through your respective attorneys. That matters not. What you're after is the final agreement you can live comfortably with.

Be prepared to start with the standard lease the landlord hands you and go from there. Look it over and decide which clauses you are comfortable with and which are unacceptable. Decide which you can object to and then give in on, and which will cause you to walk away. By conceding some points, you may be able to make others stick. A lot depends on who you're dealing with. Psychology works on some people, but not all. Just don't lose sight of what you're after!

Let me repeat. You may be willing to go along with everything that's in that standard or customized lease. But for pity sakes, get it explained to you. *Get it explained to you by your own attorney!* Don't be afraid to ask crazy questions. You may think you're making yourself sound stupid when you do, but it's your money you're spending. It's your future you're playing with. Get your money's worth.

Keep the last paragraph in mind if you decide to buy. There are far more hazards in a property purchase than there are in a lease. Since buying a bit of the old sod is more familiar to most of us, I'll not go into quite as much detail about the basic mechanics. Even if you're a neophyte, you'll find the procedure is generally stylized and a proscribed ritual prevails.

I will stress the point that all of the cautions concerning renting also apply to buying, be it raw land or improved. Restriction requirements, zoning, parking, commercial codes, the whole mess of twisted red tape are there for you when you deal with your own property. Do your homework.

When purchasing unimproved land you intend to build on, it might be a good idea to find out just what that land is composed of. Was it a landfill 40 years ago that will suddenly start leaking explosive or toxic fumes about the time you move in? Is the soil stable enough to hold your building over the years?

If you're buying an existing structure for remodeling, is the foundation strong enough to bear the additional weight you're going to load onto it? Can the floors hold up a dental chair without sagging? Is the site a swamp after a really heavy rain? Or will that lovely terraced hillside behind you end up in your back door some soggy morning? Is your title subject to reserved rights? (It's most disconcerting to find an oil rig in your back yard when you return from vacation!)

All of these things have happened to others. History could repeat itself if you're not wary.

Of prime importance is financing. Gramps might've been able to walk into a bank and trot out in minutes with oodles of green with no more collateral than his dental degree. It doesn't work that way any more. Therefore, the first place you need to go is to the bank or other lending source to see just how viable your dream is.

Go prepared even though this is a preliminary scouting expedition. It'll save you a lot of sleepless nights later on. If you wait until you've committed to a spot, panic time may set in and coerce you into a less favorable borrowing situation.

Have a reasonably concrete financial plan you can hand the lender. It should show about what you think you can comfortably manage in the way of debt, realistic figures to support your contention and a credit history which includes more than a car note and a marginally past due credit card bill.

Assuming you have credible assets, spend a few dollars having an accountant work up a financial statement for you. Don't just fill in one of the bank's pre-printed forms! Though the final figures may be the same, the custom report is more impressive.

Add to your documentation copies of your last several year's income tax statements. If there's a member of your family or a responsible friend who'll back you by co-signing your note, have that in writing-along with something showing a bit of the cosigner's credit history and net worth.

It sounds like a lot of paper just to obtain a possible—repeat, possible—favorable view of your tentative proposal. The fact is bankers and other commercial lenders like lots of paper. The thicker the file, the easier it is for them to point to it if the loan goes sour. They can moan that it had to be a good deal with all that supporting data. It gets them off the hook. It's sad, but it's possible the deciding factor in your obtaining a loan is the number of inches of 20-pound bond you stack up on the lender's desk.

Don't make an appointment at just one bank. Visit all you have time for. Though they're becoming rare, I personally prefer the small bank that's not a branch of a national concern. The loan officer you talk to usually has greater latitude to make an initial judgment about where you stand. In the large bank, your proposal will have to go through several review processes for any decision, something that may take weeks.

There are other alternatives to raising money besides the traditional bank or savings and loan. Insurance companies will sometimes underwrite a property purchase and subsequent construction. Dental associations may have contacts with underwriters that look favorably on dental office financing. The business section and sometimes the classified ads in the local newspaper have small notices of people who want to lend money. One of your classmates or other colleagues may have sources they've tapped in the past.

I'd caution against borrowing heavily from relatives. There are two problems associated with this route to capital. First, some kin may feel they've bought the right to butt into your business and virtually run it. Second, the family blowup that could occur if you miss a payment next year. Only Heaven itself can heal some of the schisms that have occurred when a relative defaults on a note. If you feel you must tap good old Aunt Harriette, do so knowing the added risks you may be taking. Auntie may not be that smiling, benevolent soul you think she is when her loot is on the line!

The real estate agents who shows you property may have sources of money you couldn't easily access on your own. If they think it's the only way they can sell you what they've convinced you is right for you, they may even twist the owner's arm to finance the deal personally. In a fairly slow market where the property's been sitting a while, you might be able to obtain more favorable terms this way than you would from a more conventional lender.

A warning about financing. If your reserves are so meager that you must finance part of a raw land purchase, you may well have troubles with construction financing. Your initial lender's not about to give up any first mortgage rights. Whoever puts up the money for subsequent substantial additions or improvements will not look favorably on having to run the added risk of a second mortgage. Even if they do, your interest rate on the second mortgage will be significantly higher.

If your selection has not transferred ownership for a sufficient number of years, you may be able to avoid duplicating title insurance costs by simply having your attorney check the title. If you pay for title insurance, this investigation will be done anyway and someone has to pay for it. A new title policy will be required by any future lender when you borrow against the place. Why buy twice or even thrice? The same holds true when buying a building for subsequent renovation.

I will offer a full disclaimer, however. See what your attorney has to say about the advisability of this action. Make him or her take a few minutes and explain exactly how title insurance works. What works well in one state may not be smart in another.

When buying a building for remodeling, you need the services not only of an attorney, but a contractor and a first-class building inspector. Even if an inspection is required in your state as a part of title transfer or is customary practice expected by a lender, get your own independent evaluation.

You need to know precisely what you're buying in relation to using it as an office. Nothing is quite as disconcerting as finding out that partition you wanted moved must stay where it is to keep the roof from falling in. It's equally bad to discover the plumbing will have to be replaced because it doesn't meet a new code. It may be OK for it to be used in exactly the way it is now, but changes may require a whole new system.

If you feel ill prepared to navigate solo through the shoals of negotiating a purchase, there is one helpful development in recent years that may offer hope. That is the buyer's-specialty real estate broker who'll do the dirty work for you.

Unlike the traditional broker or agent, this is an individual you hire specifically for the purpose of looking out for your interests. For a fee or commission, they'll do all the negotiating, haggling, arranging loans, finding inspectors, and more.

They are responsible only to you, not the seller. If your deal involves a decent chunk of change, these individuals may quickly pay for themselves by saving you not only money, but valuable time. You may find one of this new breed of agents through the yellow pages or by asking the local real estate association. If your attorney is familiar with the ins and outs of real estate, he or she may be able to make a recommendation.

The bottom line on all this is, the buyer must be wary. There are legal protections to be had when things go sour, but they take time, money, and energy that could better be spent in rehabilitating teeth. It may be a cliché, but the ounce of prevention still matters!

# Chapter 8

# Purchasing A Practice

Once you've decided to strike out on your own, a number of different routes are readily available in addition to starting from scratch.

You can buy a practice outright. You can ease into an existing practice by becoming an associate with an agreement to form a partnership or take over in a given amount of time. You can initially jump in as a partner in a going practice. You and one or more colleagues can start your own partnership or group. You may become the sole owner of an existing practice, retaining the seller as an associate. You can form a loose arrangement within an established practice on a space sharing basis. Only your imagination and that of the established dentist/seller limits the possibilities.

When you look at all the listed options, and possibly others, it becomes obvious there are comparative advantages to each. What is not quite as obvious is the things they have in common.

There's a waiting patient pool. All of the equipment necessary to work efficiently is in place. There's a trained staff functioning daily which presumably knows the needs and quirks of the patients. There's an immediate cash flow. There are no hassles trying to negotiate leases and permits. In many instances, there's less initial financial outlay.

This does *not* mean there are no detractions. Let's look at some of those very briefly. There's more detail on most of them later on.

The equipment in the practice you're planning to buy may be old, unsightly, inefficient, or just plain worn out. The usual problem here is that your available cash or line of credit may not stretch to handle the additional cost required to upgrade. Sometimes there's a psychological drawback in the patients' minds, too. They may think all that fancy new equipment might mean their bill's about to require a trip to the bank for a second mortgage on their homestead. They might even be correct.

The staff may not suit your needs in temperament, work habits, or appearance. While this may be an indication you've picked less than the perfect practice, it could also mean your predecessor hadn't hired wisely and was too poor a manager to fire the lot of them. I refer you to later pages for a more complete discussion of this problem.

The premises may be in need of serious renovation— something the present owner may be blind to or purposely ignoring. Again, you're faced with the same dilemma you saw concerning outmoded equipment.

The expensive pile of supplies and unusable equipment novelties tucked away in a closet somewhere might not be what you're comfortable with. The chapter on evaluation looks at this smaller difficulty.

The office may be tied into an alternative treatment delivery scheme that isn't generating net income commensurate with the amount of work required. The better paying alternative schemes may not be transferable. You may find you're being asked to buy something that won't be there when you take over!

For these and many more reasons, you need to look far beyond the normal superficial seller's analysis of a practice to dig out what's really there. Equally important is what's not there! This is entirely up to you to do. Specifics will follow later.

For now, let's look more generally at what's involved in entering an existing practice, starting with unearthing the most suitable situation. For simplicity's sake, I've made the focus of the discussion a simple buyout. The principle's the same for all other arrangements, though.

There are a couple of obvious routes to take in finding a practice. Probably the most common is the practice broker. They're not difficult to locate because they advertise in nearly every journal specific to the area you're interested in. You may also find them manning booths at conventions and meetings. A few make it a point to contact graduating classes at the various universities. Some schools and dental societies may maintain lists of brokers working in the area you're interested in. The trusty full-service supply house may be of help, too.

Last, but not necessarily least, are your colleagues practicing in the general area. They may have knowledge of the reputation of one or more of these individuals or companies. They may also be aware of the reputations of these agents, something that might save you a great deal of time and money.

The next most common place to find a practice for sale is in the classified asvertisement section of journals. JADA has a fair listing of practices available, especially in areas that aren't well served by a regional, state, or local publication. Some state societies maintain a referral service, as do a few universities. Some make a nominal charge for this service, but some do not.

Once again, the supply house may serve as a good referral source.

Most rare and least reliable is the "word-of-mouth" route, although when it works, it works well. This ancient and much maligned informal network may be of value in locating opportunities that are extremely new. Visiting a few colleagues offices in your projected area may lead you to someone who's just at that moment ready to put a practice on the market. A bit of handshaking during the social hour at a local dental meeting may prove profitable.

The advantage of going through a broker is having a lot of the leg work done for you. Myriad facts and figures about the practice are assembled, giving you a preliminary overview of the condition the office is in. A few phone calls will generally fill your mailbox with details of practices in the area you've decided on.

Before going further, I shall emphatically repeat the warning given when discussing real estate agents. Most practice brokers are primarily in business to make money selling practices. A few do round out their income by acting as management consultants, but by and large, they make their living out of practice sales.

They're out for a buck just as we all are. They want to sell a practice to you in the worst way—and sometimes that's the way they do it! They are, with rare exceptions, being paid by the seller, just the way it works in a real estate transaction. *And don't you forget it!*

A few enterprising brokers have figured out how to play both ends of the deal, charging both the seller and buyer a fee. This presents an obvious conflict of interest. If such a situation arises, be firm and negotiate the total package price down to compensate for your added expense. Better still, refuse to pay this lug if at all possible. If a broker asks for an up-front fee to represent you in a transaction where he or she has any financial interest in assisting the seller in making a sale, make haste toward the nearest high ground while you still have title to your shirt!

The only exception to this dictum is the instance where you hire a broker as a consultant to run interference for you. If you do so, avoid making his or her fee based on the sales price. An hourly charge is acceptable. A flat fee is ideal.

Another caution. In some states, practice brokers are either poorly regulated or not regulated at all. In these areas, the only thing a broker absolutely needs to be in business is a phone and the listing of a practice for sale. Some states require they be licensed as real estate agents or brokers, but some don't. I mention this to emphasize there's no real recognized national industry standard of behavior imposed by law or custom on some of these people.

This is not an indictment of their profession. Most are sincere, honest, motivated, hard workers. For some, selling practices is merely one facet of a general commercial business brokerage and all that inefficiency is due to a lack of expertise.

I will give you a point of information to file in your memory bank when dealing with a broker. Kindly remember dentists place high on the sucker lists of con men, used car dealers, and telephone stock sellers—a fact not unknown to devious people only somewhat less crass. One might be that smiling broker with the great stories!

In negotiating your deal through a third party or directly without a broker, you'll find you're about to spend a considerable amount of time hunched over a calculator or the spreadsheet section of your trusty computer. Masses of raw information must be digested and analyzed to see if you've found a bargain, a good deal, or a shortcut to bankruptcy. Don't expect to rush through this process, either. Your future probably depends on it.

What information do you need to know concerning a practice? The answer is, *everything*. Many of the highlights are provided by an analysis drawn up for the seller, but a lot of solid information isn't. If you're into a do-it-yourself sale, it's up to you to ferret out most of the details. For now we'll leave the financial aspects alone and stick to the more general considerations you should be aware of. Let's begin with that old familiar friend, location.

Everything that's already been said about checking a physical location, with the possible exception of the portion of the chapter that discusses the mechanics of renting, buying, or building, should apply. The only thing different is, you do the process in reverse. You start with the specific location and work your way outward to the more general.

Why bother? After all, it's a going practice. The selling doctor is making money. So what? The fact a practice has been in existence for some time in one spot doesn't mean that's the spot for you five years hence, or even now. The current dentist has built up patient loyalty over a period of time. Those patients might stick with him even if the location has deteriorated to the point of being downright putrid. Whether they'll proffer you that same consideration is highly problematic.

You'll be, after all, an unknown quantity. Simply buying the practice and receiving, at best, a standard glowing recommendation from their old and trusted dentist may help, but many patients who are not fanatically attached to your predecessor may very well opt for greater convenience elsewhere.

That brings up an interesting conundrum. If you find a great practice, fantastic from your standpoint, and with terms most agreeable, should you grab it and plan on moving to a better office immediately?

The answer is definitely not. No matter how miserable the situation, you're going to have to put up with it for a while if you buy. Patients are drawn into a practice that presents a total package, not just the doctor, although he or she is routinely the deciding factor. There are two things remaining when their doctor is gone—the help and the location.

When you buy that practice, you're tearing them away from their doctor. He or she has been their dental security blanket. Losing that security is enough shock for the time being. Don't pour large doses of concentrated sodium chloride solution on their fresh abrasion by jerking the familiar surroundings away, too. Not even when they're miserable digs!

How long should you stay put in this situation? This is a tough question to answer with any conviction, since there's no general formula that will apply to all practices. It depends to a great extent on what percentage of the patient roster you see in a given time.

As an example, consider an orthodontist. In something like six months nearly all the active patients will have been treated several times. The transfer of loyalty will have taken place. Moving will be no problem.

For a general practitioner, getting your hands in all the mouths you're likely to see will take several years, perhaps as much as four in some cases. Changing locations in anything less than two years would be a risk.

One exception would be the involuntary move—the "lost-the-lease" situation. If you feel you absolutely must move before you've acquainted yourself with all the patients you're likely to transfer, this ploy could be used to generate a bit of sympathy at your being evicted and thus possibly overcoming some of the negative aspects of the move.

Even with this approach it's still a chancy thing. You're better off sticking where you are for a while. Incidentally, I leave it to you to decide the ethics of utilizing such a deception.

Once you've established in your own mind you can live with the location, it's time to hone in on the other two mainstays of the practice. The doctor and the assistants.

It doesn't matter which you tackle first since they're equally important. In some situations it's best to concentrate primarily on the help. In others, the doctor is the one to spend the most time on. For discussion purposes only, let's start with the help.

The various assistants in a practice probably know more about what's really going on in an office than the high-and-mighty doctor. This is especially true if they've been there a while. The difficulty in prying out information is they're torn between loyalty to their boss and the self-serving desire to make a good impression on you, their potential future employer.

Don't expect to have them open up in 10 minutes. It takes time. For this reason, clear their absence from their duties with the boss before you spirit them away. His schedule may not allow your interruptions, especially one of this magnitude, without a significant advance warning. The last thing you want to do is make the boss mad when you're trying to buy the practice he's operating!

I repeat myself: Clear the absence of the help with the boss!

This may sound like I'm suggesting kidnapping them. Not quite, although in some instances it might be the quickest way to the truth. I'm merely recommending you don't grill them in the confines of the office.

Why? Walls have ears. Confidences may be harder to come by. There are also interruptions. It's too easy for someone else to pop in to ask Susie where she hid the irreplaceable office widget. If at all possible, find neutral territory to conduct your interviews. A nonthreatening environment like a restaurant is ideal if it's one where there aren't many customers in between rush hours.

For a man interviewing a woman, or a woman interviewing a man, avoid any situation that might present even the slightest suspicion of anything other than a purely business intent. Places like hotel or motel rooms, or lobbies of the same when you're staying there, are worst. Equal no-nos are bars and secluded spots where there isn't a lot of light or traffic nearby.

Your best bet is to let the interviewee pick the place within the general parameters of reasonable privacy and lack of interruption. Above all, do not ask for an interview outside of the normal office hours. You'll usually meet with resentment and hostility right off the bat. Naturally, if the interviewee suggests it, it is permissible. But be sure the location meets the above criteria. Your interviewee may have an agenda, too.

Do you pump them individually or in groups? There are things to be said for both methods. Some professional interviewers prefer group discussions and have great success this way prying out strengths and weaknesses in a business.

For the amateur, I'd suggest the one-on-one discussion. There are several reasons for this. First, you have a good chance to appraise the individual you're talking to without the conversation being dominated by someone else. Since you're possibly going to be working closely with these people, the better you know them, the better off you are. And vice versa.

Additionally, you remove the chance of accidentally pitting two antagonists against one another. In case you didn't know it, dental offices can be hotbeds of rivalry and jealousy. In fact, it's hard to find one where there isn't at least a smidgen of resentment somewhere!

Unrest in a dental office? Definitely! When there are two or more employees, there's jealousy. The larger the staff, the more intense the inter-office politics. Assistants routinely resent receptionists who dictate the work load they have. Receptionists resent assistants who have the ear of the doctor throughout the day. They both hate the hygienist who usually has the luxury of setting her own agenda. They all hate the office queen bee who rules the hive, often without the doctor being fully aware of it.

These little intramural power games that go on in every office are something you need to be aware of. A moderate amount of this interplay is normal. Not even the best-regulated office is immune. If it's excessive, there's trouble brewing.

Skillful questioning will eventually unearth the intensity of the infighting. The level may be as important to the smooth running of an office as the office manual. If you're reasonably lucky, by the time you finish talking to all the help, you'll have a fair profile of everyone in the office, including personal attitudes.

A hint. A couple of doctors I've met tried this tactic with a tape recorder on the table. What they got was about as valuable as Monopoly money at the corner grocery. Any attempt at note taking will be equally counterproductive. If need be, make notes or some other record of your impressions immediately after the interview. Just don't do it in the presence of the interviewee!

What other issues should you consider important? For now, learn the general level of job satisfaction. While pay and benefits are things employees are interested in, they seldom put them down as primary reasons for continuing to work at, or leaving a job.

Ask each employee to assess the overall functioning of the office. What can be improved? What habits or attitudes does the doctor have that limit the success of the practice? Ditto for other members of the staff. What changes could be made to increase the production and revenue without compromising the overall patient satisfaction? What are the most common patient gripes?

What gripes does this particular staff member have?

A minor point. The longer the assistant's been in the practice, the more information she or he has stored, and conversely, the more loyalty probably acquired. Don't take everything you're told at face value. Each individual will have a personal hatchet to hone.

Phrasing questions so they require open-ended answers will elicit more information than a multiple choice test or a "yes/no" format. If you're in the least hesitant about your interviewing skills, take time to read a book or two on the general technic. The local library's full of them.

The bonus for preparing yourself this way is twofold. You'll get more information immediately, and the skills you gain will help later in dealing with your patients.

Ideally, what you're looking for is the well-run, reasonably friction-free office. If there are bits and pieces of discord, try to learn what or who is responsible. That way you may be able to isolate the situation or an abrasive individual and eliminate the problem early on. If there's too much interoffice pettiness, it reflects negatively on the viability of the practice—a valuable fact to have in your arsenal at negotiation time.

Tackling talking to the doctor is entirely different. Your visits are directed by totally separate circumstances than your chats with the help. You need to beard this lion in his own den since that self-same den is what you're after. The lion's behavior there is paramount to your understanding of the practice.

I urge you to use caution. This man is on his best behavior while you're around. He'll be nicer to the help, to his patients, to salesmen, telephone callers, and small children than he normally is. Granted, there may be exceptions to this dictum, but most dentists in this situation feel they're on stage. They're giving the performance of their lives, hoping to be well paid for it.

Because of this, the questions you ask are different. Try to ascertain why the practice is for sale. The reason may not be exactly what is offered for public consumption. Learn, if possible, the doctor's real attitude toward the practice, the patients, and the whole concept of dentistry in today's not-so-brave new society. These intangibles will color the man's approach to his practice, something you're vitally interested in.

One note of interest and something you should be aware of. The doctor you're dealing with is selling you a piece of his life. That practice is his baby, his child, and possibly the big love of his life. He has nurtured it through sick times and watched it grow. His life is inexorably bound up within the confines of the walls surrounding that equipment.

In the depths of his subconscious, you're a potential interloper, something akin to the questionable suitor who wants to spirit away his baby daughter princess. No matter how sick he may be of the practice of dentistry—or how sick he might be physically—selling his practice is tantamount to parting with a big piece of his existence. It may be a love-hate relationship, but it's all his. The same thing applies to assistants if they're long in the practice. Their attachment may be even greater than that of the doctor. They may not only be in love with the practice, they may have a strong emotional attachment to the doctor himself. How that affects the way they look on you is anybody's guess.

They may root for you since you're supposedly helping the doctor in achieving his wishes, or they may do their best to sabotage you at every turn for helping the doctor abandon them. Be on guard.

If you keep this in mind, you'll understand how it's possible for negotiations to go awry over a truly trivial point. It's much like a divorce in which mammoth arguments are generated between the principals by something as insignificant as a favorite paring knife. You may find giving on small points of contention will allow you to make a much better overall arrangement.

A seemingly belligerent or intractable mind-set on the part of the seller may be apparent early. If you're among the first to look at the practice, you may sense an ambivalence in the seller's attitude. This is usually not a reflection on you. It's no more than the seller being suddenly faced with the concrete realization of what's about to happen. When it hits him, it may hurt.

It should be obvious that if you're the first in line for the practice, negotiation will be harder. The ideal situation is to be low down in a fairly long line of basically uninterested "lookers." By that time, reality may have set in. The seller may finally understand he's not going to get everything he wants. He may also agree to more generous financing terms, or change his mind about insisting on cash.

On the flip side, those others may have spotted a major flaw in the practice that made it unattractive. The longer it's been on the market, the more wary you should be.

So how do you approach this stranger? For your first contact, try to steer the talk away from the assets and glowing, possibly rehearsed, sales pitch. You're a long, long way away from the negotiation stage. In fact, you should be a long way from even thinking about the final outcome. For now you should be concentrating on learning enough about the doctor himself to see if you're the one to step into his well-polished loafers with minimal pain and adjustment.

The doctor you're talking to may have other ideas. Whatever the reason for the sale, this will be that doctor's biggest selling job of his career. Every dime he's able to wheedle out of you is pure profit. Indeed, his retirement or move to set up another practice somewhere else may well hinge on his ability to grab top dollar. Don't you forget it!

What you're looking for most at this time is a personality and attitude meld between the two of you. Ideally, his beliefs and yours should be more than just similar. This agreement should extend well beyond the narrow subject of your mutual profession.

You should feel you're standing in front of a mirror of your own feelings and thoughts. You should be able to predict with some degree of accuracy what his answers will be before you finish posing a question. While this probably won't occur, look for it anyway. The closer you two are in this regard, the more the practice is suited to you.

Why? When you purchase a practice, you're primarily buying an elusive, indefinable "goodwill." The main ingredient of goodwill is a patient base. Consider what this truly means. The patient base is there because of that particular doctor's attitude and method of patient approach. He's worked hard to gather in those mouths that feed him so well.

Change is one thing patients don't like. Especially if they don't initiate it. The more you're a clone of the dentist they're used to, the better. Monstrous dislocations in the practice philosophy or outlook will mean monstrous defections of that fragile patient base to other offices.

What if the practice is an estate sale where the doctor is either deceased or declared incompetent? Fear not. There are ways around actually meeting your predecessor. A thorough review of 25 to 50 patient files will assist in telling you something of the doctor's outlook toward his patients. If there's an assistant or two still on the premises, they can help considerably in explaining what the office actually did for patients—and how they went about it.

It may take a couple of visits for you to fully delve into the attitude of the seller. Don't rush too fast. Being too eager may weaken your future negotiating strength.

The exception is an estate sale or a forced sale where the office is either closed or open only minimal hours under the direction of a temporary replacement. Treat any office where the principal doctor is not on the scene as an emergency sale, no matter how well his absence is being covered by others.

Haste is in order to help maintain as much of the patient base as possible. As I pointed out previously, patient loyalty is a most fragile commodity. Use your best judgment as to how fast you need to proceed.

If, after these initial interviews, what you've learned hasn't dissuaded you from pursuing the matter further, it's time for the dirty work of figuring out just what that practice is really worth. In short, it's time to get your hands dirty!

# Chapter 9

# Evaluating A Practice, General Considerations

In this and the following chapters we'll look at how to evaluate a practice to see if it's feasible for you to buy it. Your goal is to pay for it without having to exist for the majority of your professional life on stale crackers and subsidy cheese. We'll also look at how the mix of figures and facts presented to you will help you determine if it's the right practice for you psychologically.

To save you time writing down all the necessary items discussed here, there's a list of them at the back of the book. There are also a few comments along the way that'll help you put what you're analyzing in perspective.

When a broker, or more rarely the seller, presents you with a prospectus concerning a practice, there are pages and pages of glowing accolades and a batch of fancy figures justifying the final asking price. Part of the stuff you can trust and part of it you can't. Because you don't know which is which, you have to re-check everything!

The first thing to discard is any projection of the practice's future. This is nothing but fortune-telling at its worst. I know. I've prepared some for clients and analyzed others. It's an expected part of the total sales pitch. It does have one use which will be discussed later. For now, forget it.

Why? There's no way to tell what sort of a gross increase, if any, a dental office will produce in six months, much less in three or four years, or longer. It's even more chancy if there's a change in ownership.

By way of explanation, the projection is routinely derived from one of two premises. The first is that the practice gross receipts will continue to grow at the same rate they have for the past few years. In many cases this is no more than what would be expected from increased fees due to inflation. Naturally, this isn't mentioned.

The second method is to take the last year's gross and apply a fixed rate of increase to it to arrive at the next year's projection. This is then repeated for succeeding years. The bottom line grows like compounded interest on money you don't have—and is worth about the same amount.

The next item to set aside is the description of the area in which the practice is located. This is routinely nothing more than a combination of facts and figures obtained from a collection of World Almanacs, Chamber of Commerce brochures and maybe the Census Bureau. This takes less than 30 minutes to prepare and can be done without setting foot within 1,000 miles of the city in question.

A couple of phone calls, a trip to the trusty bookshelf, and you're home free. I assure you, no one trying to sell a practice is about to advertise that the dream spot is in the middle of a perpetual smog alert that requires you to ride a bicycle the last 30 blocks to the office. Do your own assessment if you're serious about the practice.

The first thing you do look at seriously is whatever passes for an annual statement. Most are now being generated either by accountants or computers. Either way, you have your work cut out for you. It'll take a lot of pencil pushing to plow through a mass of that stuff.

A generic note. Many of you will find some of the following a bit elementary. I assure you, many of your colleagues have missed one or more of these obvious things when they've tried to make sense out of what they're handed. If you feel I'm insulting your intelligence by going back to beginning math, I'm sorry. Bear with me—one of your classmates needs help.

There are some points of difference in the way figures are handled in a practice that's incorporated when compared to one that's not. Take heart. The raw data is there if you dig long enough.

The first figure you're after is gross production for each of the last three years. There's a small catch here. Did the nature of the practice change in those three years? It'll fudge the figures, sometimes drastically.

Here's an example. Was a contract with an HMO, PPO, or other alternative delivery scheme instituted or cancelled during that time? Was the nature of the contract changed? What percentage of the gross came from this change?

If the practice is strictly a traditional fee-for-service one, production is a straightforward figure. You're home free. If there's an alternative delivery component, you have to do some adjusting to get a true picture.

Depending on the bookkeeping system, you'll need some deductive reasoning to break out those special figures and place them in proper perspective. It's vitally important to know what percentage of the total production is being discounted in one way or another to a commercial payer. The "why" will become apparent in a moment.

For now let's simply take the raw production total, work with it, and see what it will tell us. The most elementary exercise is to divide it by the number of hours worked and arrive at an hourly rate of return the office is generating. It's simple enough. Add up the hours marked off in the appointment book for an average week, multiply by the weeks worked and divide it into the production figure.

Again, a catch. Let's turn to the appointment book. You should have a copy of at least a couple of representative months from the previous year. If you can get your hands on the whole year's book, so much the better. The reason for this is, both monthly production and days worked may vary widely throughout the year. Further, that month or two you've been given may not be typical. Remember, the seller is putting his dominant foot out in front.

Here are examples. All doctors tend to forget those long weekends they take off when figuring how many hours a year they work. The dentist who claims he/she takes no more than the customary two week vacation may well sneak off for a total of another week or two for seminars, legal holidays, office party time at Thanksgiving, Christmas, New Years, etc.

You may find the true per/hour charge is greater than listed. This is a nasty little secret you can keep to yourself and chortle over. (That is, unless you plan on being absent an equal amount of time your first couple of years in the practice.) If the seller was aware of this rosy figure, he might want to renegotiate the selling price. Upward.

You may have discovered in your interviews with the assistants that they have to routinely work half their lunch hour and another half hour after the posted office hours. This often adds as much as four hours a week to the presumed time schedule.

It doesn't sound like much, but it can add up to several hundred hours a year. When you figure the average dentist claims to put in 1,500 hours a a year, it makes a big change in the hourly rate you're after. I've found some dentist's estimates are off by as much as 20 to 30 percent.

Incidentally, while it doesn't have much to do with purchasing a practice, that 1,500-hour figure is overly generous in most cases. You'd be closer to the truth if you said 1,200 potential productive hours.

Be that as it may, the resulting hourly figure you come up with after making your adjustments is interesting, but what good is it? Right now it's just one more figure for you to balance in your head. Let's therefore take it one step further.

Go back to the appointment book and look for holes, such as cancellations and unfilled time slots. See how many hours a month everyone's idle. While this can be time for doing book work, dictating notes, cleaning drain traps, pouring impressions or other non-income producing work, there are a couple of things you should be aware of.

The first is obvious. This affects the effective hourly rate you just came up with. Cutting this "time lost" factor will increase revenue potential without increasing the fee charged to the patient.

Lost time also indicates to an extent the efficiency, and conceivably, the current viability of the office. A lot of holes in that book mean either gross inefficiency or a practice that may be in some serious trouble.

The latter may need a bit of explanation. A young practice, under five years old, is presumably still growing. Vacancies in the book are to be expected. In the older, more mature practice it means there's too much competition, a failure on the part of the doctor to continue to recruit new patients, a failure to sell patients on necessary or advisable treatment, a general complacency or downright disinterest in the practice, or a combination of these and other factors. The reason needs to be looked into to see if it's correctable.

This hourly charge figure is valuable for another reason. If you take the idle time and multiply it by the hourly rate you've just established, you get a fair approximation of the absolute maximum annual production this office is capable of without changing anything else.

There's another catch. You won't work at the same rate as the dentist who's in charge now. You need to translate it into your own production potential in this office. It'll take a bit of time, but it's simple.

Go back to the appointment book and see how long it takes the seller to do the various common procedures. For example, if he takes an hour and a half to do a crown preparation that only takes you an hour, there's the possibility you can increase the production total without significant change in basic overhead. Naturally, the reverse is also true.

Take a typical week or two out of the book and figure how much more or less dentistry you might produce, using the same mix of patient procedures listed. Multiply the additional hours available per year by the hourly rate and add or subtract it from the adjusted production potential.

*Evaluating A Practice, General Considerations*

   This tells you what your potential limit is in the practice. You can use the percentage change to alter the initial figure to determine where you would stand if you were doing exactly what the selling dentist did. If your figure's considerably lower than the seller's, it points out your relative ability to make a living and pay off the purchase price.

   Yet another word of warning here. You have to remember how the seller handles his patients. If he routinely spends a half hour chatting with them, you'll have to do about the same thing or risk alienating a fair percentage of the clientele.

   This is an extreme example, but it illustrates the point. There may be a theoretical untapped potential on paper that won't translate out in the real world. In this instance, increasing efficiency might very well cost you big money.

   The next item you should look at is the one labelled "gross receipts." If you're investigating a corporate report, be sure you don't pick up the gross income figure. They can vary significantly. Accountants have a nasty habit of slipping things around to alter the final result that's presented to the Internal Revenue Service. It's perfectly legal, but it can confuse us poor, uninitiated dentists if we're not careful.

   Compare the gross receipts to the gross production figure you first looked up. Calculate the percentage of collection for each of the years you have figures for. If there's a big discrepancy from year to year, find out why. If it's more than just income shifting for tax purposes, there may be a weakness.

   If the overall collection figure for the three years averages out to less than 94 or 95 percent, there's probably room for improvement. Below this figure indicates significant collection problems the doctor hasn't addressed. Most new dentists find collections are more difficult when they start out, so listen to the warning bells.

   As noted earlier, many practices are now a mix of traditional and alternative delivery methods. Very few offices keep detailed records of precisely what income comes from what source. It certainly doesn't appear on many monthly reports I've seen.

   Worse, in an office that services several different plans, it's even rarer to find out which plan accounts for what percentage of the work done. This makes it difficult to tell exactly what's making money and what isn't.

   There may be an additional trap to snare the unwary. At least one plan I am familiar with requires the dentist to have been in that office a specified amount of time. Do not assume an insurance arrangement will automatically be transferred to you. Losing the assets represented by that account may make a practice much less valuable.

Check with the underwriting companies involved to see what the restrictions may be. Spending the small time involved in a phone call or two is much better than starving for a couple of years!

Because of these factors you need to know what percentage, if any, of the total gross receipts of your target practice are being generated by such plans. You also need to know what percentage of the normal fee is being offered through the plans. If the office participates in several different ones, each needs to be analyzed separately.

You may find a sizeable proportion of the work being done is actually delivered at, or near, cost. In some instances, the unknowing dentist may, perversely, be paying the insurance company for the privilege of participating in the scheme. Sadly, many dentists don't even know they're doing this. To protect yourself, require a detailed breakdown from the seller.

Once you've done your gross production and income analysis, the next item to tackle is the overhead. This falls into two general categories. One is fixed expense and the other is the direct cost of providing service. Most expenses are comparatively straightforward, falling into one category or the other.

You'll find a few items are mixed. One example is the telephone. Certainly the basic service charge is a fixed item, one required whether a patient is ever seen or not. Long distance charges on behalf of the patient are not. They're treatment charges.

An example would be calling an out-of-town lab to check on the progress of a partial denture. For practical purposes, though, any charge category that has a significant fixed component should be labeled fixed. It may change the overall picture slightly, but not enough to make a real difference.

It's probably simplistic to repeat such a self-evident thing, but fixed expenses go on whether you have any business or not. About the only way you can cut them is to fire some of the help or turn the heat and air conditioning off.

Some items may not occur to you off-hand. For instance, if you're buying a building, don't forget to factor in the total package including not only the mortgage itself, but the additional taxes and insurance. Some of these things may not appear in the seller's analysis.

Another item you may overlook as a fixed expense is the increased expenses you're going to have paying for the practice. This will naturally not show up in the seller's figures, but it's an item you must factor into your estimation of the worth of the practice *to you*.

It's impossible to give a range of allowable figures or percentages of gross income that you should allow for fixed expenses. Conditions vary widely from city to city and practice to practice. However, a figure of around half is fairly common.

That, of course, does not include what you'll be paying additionally for the practice. What's more important is your ability to handle this fixed overhead out of your pocket in emergencies where income drops or ceases temporarily. You should be reasonably comfortable with it.

There's one tricky item generally included in the fixed-overhead picture that confuses the issue of actual monthly outlay. That's depreciation. It's a two-edged sword. It's phantom money you never really have passing through your hands except when you go to buy a new bit of equipment. Then it becomes a big expense.

Large corporations almost always have a reserve account set up to take care of replacing worn-out assets. Dental offices don't, at least not as a rule. Whether or not it belongs in your calculations at this time is anyone's guess. I'd tend to factor it in as an actual expense even though it doesn't require writing a check each month. It provides a small cushion in case of error in your calculations.

Direct expense of delivering service is another matter. All items not attributable to fixed expense can be labeled a result of treatment rendered. Close examination may show ways of trimming these items.

For example, laboratory charges vary widely and aren't always indicative of the quality of the finished product. Purchasing by mail or buying in bulk may allow sufficient savings to materially alter the effective total overhead.

A perusal of invoices in the filing cabinet should give some clues as to potential savings that can be obtained. Be sure the reduction is not at the expense of the quality of treatment the practice is currently offering.

In corporate reports—and sometimes in unincorporated ones—you'll find the doctor listed as an employee. There are justifiable bookkeeping reasons for this. In the corporate structure, the corporation can be charged for items that are logically otherwise considered the doctor's quasi-personal expenses.

These may include life, disability, and health insurance; heavy participation in a company retirement plan; a car allowance or write-off; and the like. There may be instances where money that would normally be called profit is reallocated to members of the doctor's family. For your purposes these should be broken out of the mix.

There are a couple of reasons. With the exception of a base salary, the most obvious is that items are of dubious value to your financial structuring of the practice's purchase viability. You'll probably have other priorities.

More importantly, they have little or no bearing on the true worth of the practice. They fall more under the heading of optional fringe benefits for the seller than they do real overhead. An exception should be made if part of the package deal is to continue any of these after the sale. Then they become true overhead.

One particularly gray area in the expense ledger is the category for continuing education and associated travel expense. Though questionable at times, this can be a way to bury that ski weekend the seller loves.

Don't misunderstand—quality continuing education is vital to the continued health of any practice, but there's a fair amount of abuse going on here. Look at the figure carefully and adjust, if needed. Uncle Sam may be willing to underwrite part of that great Bermuda tan, but you shouldn't consider it part of the purchase price.

Why the concern with overhead? A wise old laboratory technician once told me it didn't matter how much money anyone took in or what was spent doing it. It was what was taken home in the coin purse at the end of the day that mattered. A homely philosophy, but pertinent. If you see a way to trim overhead in that practice you're looking at, you stand a better chance of making it pay for your risk in buying it.

After you've digested the basic money flow that fuels the practice, it's a very good idea to look at where it's really coming from. It's valuable to understand precisely what type of a practice this really is.

Many computer-generated reports will give you this information, telling you how many X-rays were taken, how many crowns were prepared, and how many prophys were done.

Alternatively, you can do a survey from the appointment book or the charts. It's a relatively simple thing, and well worth the effort.

Perhaps this bit of information should've been properly addressed in the previous chapter, but it follows logically as a part of looking at the books. The significance is reasonably clear. If you hate making dentures or refuse to do so and the practice generates 20 percent of its income from false teeth, you're either in the wrong office or you'll have to change your ways. The only other alternative is to voluntarily give up a fair chunk of the gross revenue right off the bat.

This analysis additionally pinpoints weak spots in a practice and highlights profit centers. Perhaps I'm crass to refer to the delivery of a vital professional service as a loss leader or profit center, but business is business.

Let's look at a couple of examples. In one practice I dissected recently for a dentist who was dissatisfied with her gross to net ratio, the most prevalent single item on the appointment book was "prophylaxis." The biggest single net income producer category was "crown and bridge." The following figures are representative only of that particular office and shouldn't be used as a yardstick of any practice you're looking at. They're merely an illustration of what you might find if you dig deeply.

First, the prophy bit. Almost a third of the appointments in the book were for "check-ups." For this office that meant cleaning and a quick peek to see what'd gone wrong since the last time. Two bite-wing X-rays were taken approximately every second time the patient showed. In order to accomplish the work, the doctor had a full-time hygienist and another who came in one or two days a week. One assistant was assigned more or less full time to increase their productivity.

Between the two hygienists, about 200 prophys were done each month. At $15 per child and $25 per adult, the monthly take was around $4,000. The X-rays added another $500 for a total of $4,500. No charge was made for the cursory exam.

Now $54,000 a year is nothing to sneeze at. It makes a fair start on a decent annual gross. Right? But is it good business? Not necessarily. At least not in this office. Here's what it cost that doctor to put that money in the bank.

The full time hygienist's salary, including hidden costs such as the dentist's share of Social Security and pension plan contributions, was around $3,000 a month. The part-timer averaged out something like $1,000. The assistant weighed in at $1,500. Additionally, a part-time bookkeeper was necessary to keep track of all the paperwork the two income producers generated. This cost an estimated $500.

That's not all. Supplies to support that patient load ran about a $1,000 a year. Even cleaning teeth costs something. One operatory was dedicated to the full-time hygienist. The equipment cost a conservative $10,000, or $800.00 a year. Additional rent for her space plus an annual allocation of the phone and other utilities was estimated at $1,000. The grand total yearly cost was just under $80,000.

This didn't even take into consideration the fact the part time hygienist used one of the doctor's own allocated operatories, thus potentially reducing her efficiency. Nor did it consider the wear and tear on the rest of the office caused by something like 2,500 annual bodies squirming around on the reception room chairs and scuffing the rug.

This doctor was paying out of her own pocket something over $25,000 a year just for the dubious privilege of keeping her patients clean.

Put another way, this doctor had to dedicate in excess of $60,000 of her own gross production just to offset this loss. Naturally the argument can be made that this expense could be charged to public relations, patient retention or even internal advertising. That's not germane to this discussion.

If that's the office you're looking at, knowing the loss is there will help you ascertain what improvements you might make to increase profits or decrease losses. Whether or not you do so is another philosophical discussion better left for late night bull sessions.

A quick comment before we go on to the crown part of this busy, but bumbling, office. This office was a classic case of inefficiency run well down the road toward the hamlet of Amuck. What this doctor was paying for was stroking her ego at meetings and reunions where she could brag about how busy her office was. After all, if she had two hygienists, she had to be busy, didn't she? Busy meant successful—or at least she thought so. Even when she saw the figures she stubbornly resisted making improvements!

What change was possible? In this office, the full-time hygienist worked 35 hours a week. What with doing prophys on kids as well as adults, it wouldn't be too unreasonable to expect her to struggle through two patients an hour, or 70 a week. That's 280 a month for those of you who flunked math, about 80 more than the monthly production total for both ladies.

According to my thinking, she should've had time left over to take care of the paperwork she generated. The recalls and phone reminders should've been her responsibility. There was absolutely no need for the part-time bookkeeper to do this job for her. There was even less justification for the additional part-time hygienist.

If you were buying an office like this, you could realize significant savings without ever letting the patients in on what you were doing. They wouldn't notice the increased efficiency except possibly wondering in idle moments why Suzy didn't take a half hour to chat every time they came in.

A repeated small word of caution. Merely totaling the figures doesn't always tell the whole story. If these hygienists were performing other duties that didn't show up on the books, their existence might be more justifiable. Some dentists have their auxiliaries do lengthy case presentations, for example.

Although this wasn't the case in this particular office, check before you leap to conclusions.

Now let's examine the crown-and-bridge part of our sample office. To do so we need to start with some background. This doctor worked about 1,500 hours a year, somewhat above average. The total office gross was a most comfortable $185,000, a nominal $125 an hour. But when you tally in the drag the prophy department was generating, the doctor was only considering herself worth a bit less than $80 an hour.

Our doctor produced an average of 100 units of crown and bridgework a year, roughly two a week according to an appointment book survey. This translated into a gross income of something like $50,000 a year. If you're into percentages, that's about 28 percent of the total gross income. A believer in giving her patients nothing but the very best, she paid a lab $150 a unit to do the lab work, leaving her $350 for her labors.

She meticulously took an hour and a half to prepare a tooth for a crown, an hour to pour impressions, trim and mark margins, and mount the resulting models in proper articulation before the lab ever saw them.

Seating the finished product routinely took an hour, sometimes longer. Total time, about three-and-a-half hours on average. There was a small time saving when the units were part of a bridge, but not enough to make too much difference.

Without nit-picking minor details and pennies, it looks like the fee she's charging is about right to produce the income she's generating from this service. There are savings to be had in changing to a less expensive lab and increasing efficiency in preparation and seating the finished product. This will up the hourly average, but the fee as constituted is an honest one—one a practice buyer should be able to live with. As a matter of record, this doctor's making somewhat more than her average hourly charge on this particular service.

The question then becomes—what's wrong with this picture?

The lady is taking maybe seven hours a week to produce more than a quarter of her gross income. Her hygienists are kicking in another quarter. What's she doing the other 33 hours a week? This is a practice in real trouble.

This is one that, if purchased, should be negotiated down to the bone, marrow excluded. When anyone's grossing well under $50 an hour for most of their time, they're in pretty deep. Believe me, this lady was.

There's a footnote to this story. There were three additional problems in this sample office you might be on the lookout for when you check a practice.

One, the dentist wasn't charging at all for many minor procedures she performed as a service to her patients. This was something that wasn't readily apparent without comparing patient charts with the appointment book.

Two, a great deal of time was wasted chasing into the hygienist's bailiwicks to do the freebie exam that went along with the cleaning. Fifty or so five minute interruptions a week spent with non-paying patients count up.

Three, a hidden inefficiency was a batch of small holes in the appointment book. A few were unfilled last minute cancellations the receptionist couldn't do too much about. The trouble was, some were purposely created in the hope emergencies would call, and others were there just in case our starving doctor got behind. She hated to run late and preferred to sacrifice a lot of efficiency rather than keep even one patient waiting more than a minute or two. Noble, but underproductive. Discovering things of this nature takes time. Don't rush your investigation.

When you've waded through all the fancy mathematical footwork and suffered sufficiently, you may be wondering what it all means in terms of buying a practice. I'll remind you once again that spotting possible deficiencies up front puts you into a better negotiating position when you come to the bargaining stage. You can afford to be a reasonably nice guy then while still carving out a darned good deal for yourself.

The big bonus is, if you do eventually buy the practice, you have a tremendous head start on setting things right. In the instance just outlined, eliminating the general inefficiency along with tightening up the hygienist scheduling, this practice could have the potential for a far greater gross and net—something you're looking for when checking a possible bargain.

Remember that bit of wisdom as we next explore the other side of the coin—expenses.

# Chapter 10

# The Expense Side Of The Ledger Sheet

There was some reference presented in the proceeding pages concerning the expense part of a selling dentist's evaluation. There, the viewpoint was using those expense figures in relation to the income side of the practice.

This serves to illustrate the fact that you cannot divorce the two parts of an overall picture. Though the focus now shifts to expenses as the primary target for your inspection, don't lose sight of the big picture.

There are two different places to look when considering expenses. One is the actual ledger or annual summary and reconciliation that details them. If figures aren't available from the primary source, the quickest alternative is the Schedule C of the dentist's 1040 tax form or the appropriate schedule of the corporate return.

The only drawback in depending on tax returns is that they're usually summaries. They sometimes also include questionable items which may more properly belong as an expense for the doctor, not the practice. There may additionally be a frustrating lack of detail. You'll see what I mean in a minute.

It's a good idea to look at a minimum of three year's worth of records. It's boring work and seems repetitious at times, but it's worth it. The figures tend to point the direction of the practice. Here are things to look for.

Beware of wide swings in expenses unless they can be justified. For example, there's a common practice of stacking expenses in one year for tax purposes. This is one good reason for checking several years. A clue to spotting this technique is prepayment of rent, taxes, and the like. Some doctors will even prepay their employees one paycheck, or defer payment when possible at the end of the year. Some go so far as to build up a credit in their accounts with a laboratory and supply house. It's done to shift a year's business or personal net income out of one tax bracket into another or to obtain other tax advantages.

While the tax laws in effect when this is being written don't make income shifting as enticing as it once was, it can be a useful tool when combined with the doctor's other personal income and allowable expenses. This practice may increase or decrease as tax structures change. Just be aware it's one way of unintentionally confusing the basic issues before you.

Your biggest task is to discover if there are places to cut expenses without altering service. You can't do much about the rent, but is that full page ad in the phone book all that necessary? Can you dispense with an expensive janitorial service and demean yourself by scrubbing floors a couple of times a week?

The subject of salaries is a touchy one. Normally when you buy a practice you inherit a gaggle of assistants who are probably fearful of losing their jobs even though some temporary job security may be assured in a sales agreement. As discussed elsewhere, they may be resentful of you potentially upsetting the status quo.

Any premature move on your part to dismiss one of them or adjust a single overinflated salary downward may be met with general hostility and outright sabotage. Any vague dissatisfaction they have at your taking over may erupt into open warfare if you're not very, very careful.

Need an example? Here's a true horror story. A dentist called me several years ago in tears. Real sobbing tears— unusual for a normally stoic man. He'd recently bought a practice and discovered several months later he'd somehow apparently incurred the ire of the long-time receptionist. In retaliation for whatever indignity or insult she'd suffered, or as retribution for the previous dentist abandoning her, she made it a point to call every patient she could reach.

She, in the guise of having the patient's best interest at heart, suggested they not return to the office! She went so far as to refer them to another dentist down the street. Whether she was justified in her assessment of our colleague's professional skills or not, I have no idea. His record was clean as far as I was able to ascertain. All I know for a fact is the lawyers are having a ball and my caller is trying to pay off a huge purchase price with fewer than 150 active patients!

You might find the pay scale in the office is well above normal, especially if the assistants have been with the practice some time. If the help is truly superior, that's well and good. They'll pay for themselves several times over. If they're not, let your conscience and your luck be your guide if you buy with the idea of making immediate drastic personnel or salary changes.

In specific situations, one possible way around a definite pay cut for marginal employees is the institution of a bonus plan or other similar alternate pay arrangement. This can be linked to some aspect of the performance of the office.

A few employers have been able to make office life so miserable for the target employee that they quit. This, as with other schemes to control labor costs, can backfire clear up to and including lawsuits.

There are other inventive strategies to cull or prune deadwood, but all have their perils. Be very sure you know how the affected employee or employees will react. Be equally sure of how the rest of the staff will take the news that one is on her way out the door. Remember, one of the biggest revolts ever seen in Chinese history was started by a single peasant over a dispute that amounted to what would be equivalent to about a penny today. One thing you should check carefully in relation to the help is what liabilities you'll assume as a result of your purchase. For example, it's possible you'll have to take over an unemployment insurance liability created by the seller.

There's often a fair time lapse before the rates are adjusted, so see if you'll be tagged for hidden costs. In my state at least, you buy that unfavorable record along with the assets. It may take years to clear the record! There may be other even nastier liabilities—especially if you buy a corporate structure.

Another item usually considered a fixed expense that's open to question is the cost of accounting services. Much of what's generated by these worthy individuals is a duplication of figures that can be cranked out by a decent computer program.

Often the mass of detail is unnecessary to the daily efficient functioning of a reasonably well-run dental office. The report is more impressive for its size than for its value. For many of us who struggled long and hard with only slightly advanced math, the use of double-entry bookkeeping is tantamount to slight-of-hand conjuring.

Do not misunderstand. You'll need an accountant. There are things they can do that you shouldn't even attempt. The point I'm trying to make is, you shouldn't have one doing more than is truly necessary.

Your next scrutiny should be directed toward the marketing expense item. Ask for gory details. A number of tricky things may be buried here. Gifts to friends at Christmas, donations to charity that more properly belong as a personal charge on the doctor's income tax, and reams of expensive pamphlets left unguarded in the waiting room where kids can use them to make paper planes are examples of waste or cost shifting that might be eliminated.

A small note. You may think I'm nit-picking when I point out the paper plane thing. It's true that a couple of buck's worth of brochures destroyed during a week won't break any of us. What is important is the notion that small waste should be taken care of. Enough five buck items can mount up to real cash at the end of the year.

As mentioned earlier, probably the biggest spots for fudging the figures lie in two common items  entertainment and seminars. Again, ask for detailed breakdowns of these if they are in the least sizeable. Many professionals cheerfully run the risk of incurring the ire of the Internal Revenue Service to make the office cover personal expenditures.

One outstanding example of creative bookkeeping was the doctor who put his wife on the payroll for the sole purpose of charging off all the expenses incurred when they both went on professional junkets. Her principal office duty was to stuff, lick the envelopes, stamp, and mail the monthly statements. It's a neat dodge if Uncle Sam doesn't catch on. It also juggles the books you're looking at!

Another example is the common practice of holding an open house at Christmas. This is perfectly legitimate, provided it's for patients or referring colleagues. If it's held at home where almost all the guests are friends, it becomes suspect. If it's something patients expect, you may need to continue the custom. Otherwise, let your conscience and your tax advisor be your guide. Just remember you're looking for spare change to pay off the note.

Some doctors routinely take the help along to meetings even though they'll gain little from the experience. I once met a receptionist who was totally befuddled by a highly-detailed, technical discussion of the relative merits of several methods utilized in bonding.

She ultimately spent most of the two-day diatribe at the beach, hardly a way to improve her office skills. Ski and tennis weekends for the doctor are also favorite adjuncts to meetings held in resort areas. The point is, you shouldn't count these as pure operating expense when you're figuring what it will cost you to operate the practice.

Please note I make no moral or legal judgments concerning such actions. They may in fact be quite beneficial as morale boosters for everyone. I merely point them out to alert you to dig below the surface when checking the figures you're presented. These items show how you might have an opportunity to lower present overhead without pain. The resulting savings might make purchasing that dream practice possible.

As you can see, there are generally some economies possible in any well-established office. These can be hidden in the fixed-expense section of the ledger. There are equal possibilities for pruning the expenses normally associated with treatment.

The most obvious is the lab bill. This was mentioned earlier, but more detail may help. Something as simple as pouring your own impressions can save several hundred dollars a year in even the most modest practice. As pointed out previously, lab charges should be compared. Granted, there's a quality factor involved in selecting the cheapest lab. Above that acceptable minimum quality standard, little is usually gained by going with the most expensive.

In this general area, trimming and marking your crown and bridge dies takes time, but (if you're good at it) the time saved on insertion more than makes up for it. Sometimes the net time saved allows more patients to be stuffed in the appointment book. This observation presumes you'll not be continually cursed with an overflow of patients in your new surroundings. This happy possibility will make continuing zealous frugality less necessary.

Disposable supplies may or may not be a spot to save a dollar or two. If all purchases are made through a full-service supply house, take a moment and compare representative invoices with the latest mail order catalogs. Additional savings may be had by buying in bulk if you insist on dealing with the full-service people.

One other thing you should keep an eye on. Sometimes corners are cut in the name of efficiency to the detriment of the ultimate operation of the office. If you think this is the case, make adjustments upward in your estimate of the expenses to allow for changes you'll make. Conversely, be careful the economies you intend to institute won't have the same negative effect.

As an example, the marketing budget may be minuscule in long-standing practices. You may feel that, as the new kid on the street, you'll have to extend yourself more than the present owner has. This can alter the ultimate expense bill you would face in taking over. Factor it in when deciding if this is the place for you.

Spend a little time observing the operation of the office as it relates to OSHA or other regulations. Some long-established dentists give only lip service to these rules. Indeed, their lips may move less than those of an accomplished ventriloquist! Their attitude may be downright bellicose where governmental intrusion is concerned.

While these individuals may be well able to financially afford fighting city hall if need be, you probably won't be in that position. Bringing the office into complete compliance may require both an initial outlay and significant continuing expense.

There's one area you should approach with caution. Though it's discussed elsewhere, it bears repeating here. That's the expense related to auxiliaries. Though one or more may be underworked and overpaid, grit your teeth and bear it. At least initially. Those seemingly less productive people may serve a most useful purpose. They provide the continuity in the office in the eyes of the patients. This is one place where instituting increased efficiency can cost you dearly.

There are two exceptions. One is where a long-term employee wants to retire at the same time the doctor does. Suggest strongly she do so as far in advance of your taking over as possible.

The other instance of pruning can occur in the event the seller has part of his family on the payroll. Unless they form an integral part of the office operation, deduct their salary without hesitation. Even when they do critical work, their presence may be an unsettling factor when you become the boss. Make a judgment early on and have an understanding long before the final contract is signed.

This illustrates a point. Without actually visiting and spending time in the practice, it's nearly impossible to know if an expense is justified. The seller's teen son may work his bones bare in the office while the seller's spouse is no more than an occasional roving decoration. You have to be there to judge.

This axiom of the necessity for personal observation is valid for many items in the expense ledger. Don't try to work it all out before you see what really goes on.

If you want to be efficient, you'll have a chance to observe while you check the patient files.

# Chapter 11

# The Patient Files

Patient files and charts can be extremely illuminating. They are, after all, the ultimate source of every iota of information concerning the finances and treatment, performed or emphasized in any practice. An audit is well worthwhile if you're serious about buying.

The biggest drawback is the time it takes. You'll sometimes find sellers who look on the process as an unwarranted invasion of privacy. They may also resent the inevitable disruption of the normal functioning of their office.

When doing an audit, there are several items to check. Of primary concern is the actual number of patients that can be considered active. The importance of this is obvious. The more patients there are, the more desirable, at least potentially, the practice. Indeed, some sales are based wholly or in part on this figure.

There are cautions. We'll get to them later. For the moment, your initial chore will be to confirm fairly closely the true number of files the selling dentist considers active.

Immediately the question arises—what's active? Is it those treated within the last year, two years, or three years? Or somewhere in between? The answer you and/or the seller pick will skew any results you obtain from your research.

For statistical purposes, the ADA historically said a patient was active only if he or she'd been to the dentist in the last 12 months. This was changed fairly recently. The ADA now divides active patients into two groups, those who've been treated within 12 months and those who've been absent for 12 months, but treated within 24 months.

All of the data the ADA generated prior to this change was based on annual patient utilization. Most practicing dentists long argued it was far too restrictive a definition. (Even the current definition may be suspect.) A more realistic figure lies somewhere between two and three years.

If you wish, you might divide active patients into two categories. One, those that come in routinely for their traditional semi-annual check-up. The other group would be those who don't think a six-month summons is necessary. The latter make an appointment every couple of years, generally take reasonably good care of their teeth, are loyal patients, practice boosters, and so on. They just don't feel the urgent necessity of getting their gums gouged that regularly.

Incidentally, a fair number of these folks are probably officially considered statistically by the ADA to be inactive. The nice thing is, as a practical matter they tend to balance out those who've actually left the practice but are still being carried as current patrons.

Most sellers and many practice brokers take the position the three year figure is reasonable. Most independent appraisals I've seen also tend to use this as a base. The general argument for the two year figure is that if someone hasn't seen the dentist in more than two years, he or she isn't a particularly good patient anyway and therefore shouldn't be counted. Since there are valid arguments on both sides of this fence, I suggest you take a look at what type of practice you're dealing with and make your own determination.

Suppose you're considering a children's practice a few blocks from a military base. Most of the patients are military dependents. It's reasonable to assume that if the kids don't return for two years, there's been a parental transfer which effectively removes them from the jurisdiction. In this practice, two years may be overly generous.

In a rural and somewhat isolated community where the patient's choices for treatment are fairly limited, the three year rule is completely valid. It might even be conservative. Patients in these circumstances tend to bounce from one practitioner to another, then back to the first. You might find the patients tucked away in the inactive file are more lucrative an asset than those two or three year types.

Why? The bouncers left the seller because they were dissatisfied. The alternatives may not be all that great, either. As the new available alternative, you may be just what they're looking for. They'll most assuredly give you a try!

In an orthodontic practice you have a special situation worth mentioning. Quite often only those patients under active treatment are counted. A fair

## The Patient Files

proportion of "former" patients are reasonably active for much longer than their actual treatment period. Active treatment may end after a couple of years, but retainers and checkups can go on for as much as 10 more. They'll go a long way toward paying the overhead.

Defining "active" as only those who're being currently treated would thus be a misnomer. Here, you might divide patients into three categories; those undergoing active treatment, those on a recall schedule, and those completely dismissed. A different value could be ascribed to each of the first two categories to determine the real worth of the patient base. The third category is, of course, a dead issue as far as being of any real use to you except for possibly generating a few referrals.

At the opposite end of the spectrum is the oral surgery practice. There's no such animal as an "active" patient for an oral surgeon. There's little value to a patient who hasn't been seen for *any* length of time. Realistically there's only the backlog stacked up in the appointment book that can be called active. Those massive filing cabinets may hold hordes of potential referral sources, but that's about all.

Once you've settled on a definition, the big question facing you is obvious. How do you get a reasonably accurate count of what's in the filing cabinets without going through every record? Follow along if you don't already have the answer.

Let's be very simplistic for a moment. There are two basic types of filing systems. The first is conventional storage in traditional four-drawer filing cabinets or a variation of the same. The other is the so-called horizontal system where the records are lined up on long open shelves.

With the conventional (vertical) file system, you count the number of files in one drawer and multiply by the number of drawers. In doing so you need to be aware that some drawers may be much fuller than others. If you notice a disparity, you may have to make adjustments. If you find wide variations, you may want to measure the actual lineal feet in all the drawers and treat the files in much the same way you would open horizontal files.

Working the horizontal system is a bit more straightforward. You count the files in, say, two feet of shelving and multiply by the number of two foot sections there are.

Your next step is crucial. Take a representative section of the files and examine them individually. There are several things you're looking for. The first is quite logical. How much did the dentist, the broker or the practice analyst fudge his or her figures on the number of active patients?

In the conventional system there's a hidden trap you may not spot. As just mentioned, some of the drawers may not be full. If the files have been culled recently, this is normal, but you need to be on the lookout.

If the files haven't been culled—a chore almost all front desk types hate, there may be a lot of dead pulpwood cluttering the scene. In fairness to the seller, he or she may not be aware of this fact. Few brokers or consultants doing a sales appraisal will spend the time to really check. They'll take the receptionist's word the files are active and be on their way.

For you, it's worth the aggravation and energy to go through and really confirm the figures. If the broker or analyst didn't do this, it makes a powerful argument when negotiating a more realistic sales agreement.

The next thing you should look for is the average total fee charged to these active patients and how extensive their initial treatment plans were. It's a very good idea to see what percentage of patients accepted more than minimal treatment. This tells you volumes about the true character of the practice.

Along the same lines, get a good feel for the amount of pure emergency work that's being done without follow-up. Ask yourself if this is the way you really want to practice. If this sounds like a put-down of a particular type of practice, it isn't. It's only intended to make you understand what you're thinking of buying. Remember, many highly successful practices do not fall into the traditional mold you were trained for.

By discarding those who only visit on a highly irregular or emergency basis, you can rapidly discover what the real core of the practice is. These are, in most practices, the true patients you'll have to depend on for your living. Are there enough to keep you in groceries?

I'll warn you. You don't audit files in a half an hour. A thorough perusal of a sample section may take more than a day. Why do it? The answer's simple. You're talking about what's often a six-figure investment, probably one of the biggest you'll make in your life. You're undoubtedly going into hock for years to pay it off. If you don't think it's worth a couple of days of your time to see what you're buying, you aren't ready to buy *any practice*.

The next thing you should determine is how much you think those patients are going to spend in that office in the next two or three years. Putting it bluntly, you'd be most unwise to pay a hundred dollars, plus interest, for the right to—maybe—treat a patient who's only going to drop half that much in your till over the period you're struggling to make your payments.

Another item to turn your attention to is how often fees have been adjusted during the past few years. Are the raises general or selective? How long since the last boost? For what it's worth, one of the poorer things a buying doctor can do is immediately bump fees across the board.

Patients aren't dumb. They know what they spend for the more common things they have done to their mouths. If it's been a couple of years since a good general increase, ask yourself if you can live with those skimpy fees for as much as another year.

You want to look very, very closely at the volume of past-due bills you run across. While this figure is generally available in the financial record section of any seller's proposal, it isn't always in an understandable form.

For example, the financial sheet may show a $2500 charge-off for long past-due accounts. There's no indication as to whether this is a single bad call on the seller's part in which he extended credit to one major deadbeat or whether it's a hundred $25 goofs.

The former would indicate one bit of bad judgment which can, and does, happen to all of us. The latter shows sloppy management. It could also indicate a practice that caters to small-time deadbeats, a real minus sign to tally against the stated worth of the practice.

If the appointment book doesn't reflect the number of new patients entering the practice every month, this should be checked. It's a painstaking thing to have to do, but do it if you must. This bit of information is vital to determine whether the practice is still growing, stationary, or beginning to shrink.

Here are the details. Since it's estimated that every practice loses up to 20 percent of its patients every year, you can readily see how necessary it is to attract replacements. This loss, by the way, won't necessarily show up on the financial ledger for a year or more. The file analysis is your early warning system for spotting latent trouble.

There may be other things you'll be able to discover when you go through the files. Information such as the length of time an average patient stays in the practice, changes in practice philosophy over the years, number of second or third generation families that stick with the practice and more.

These are minor points. While they may well prove valuable as marketing tool indicators later on, they don't have a great impact on the subject of the net worth of the practice. Go after these secondary bits of interesting trivia only if you have time.

One final thought. Most dentists who are hitting retirement age started practice in an era where record keeping wasn't a top priority. Practicing defensively was unheard of. A lot of very good practitioners never got the hang of adequate and highly-detailed record keeping. Don't be aghast if you run across skimpy notations done in hasty shorthand. Just plan on starting over.

This lapse on the seller's part doesn't necessarily mean future trouble for you. You might be able to use recreating those records properly as a marketing tool to nail down shaky patients. If they haven't experienced a thorough exam for some time, the process generally creates a great first impression.

This is a sneaky way of reminding you to never forget while you're checking things out to look for opportunities to make that old practice grow!

CHAPTER 12

# DECIDING IF A PRACTICE IS REASONABLY PRICED

By now you've gone through practically all the seller's records and probably have a better, more intimate working knowledge of the practice than he does. The staff is sick of your face and disruptive intrusion. The doctor is about to throw you out on any convenient portion of your anatomy as an unwelcome pest who'll never come to grips with reality enough to come up with an offer. It's now time to make the final decision as to whether you can afford the practice, whether it'll pay for itself, if it's fairly priced, and most importantly, determine whether you really want it.

Let's stop right here and gain a bit of perspective about the term "sales price" and its relationship to the entire agreement. In addition to the single figure, there are other terms to consider. What will be the down payment? What is the interest rate? What length does the payment period cover? Will the seller finance? Will a higher sales figure and lower interest rate be better, or just the opposite? What portion of the practice is exceptionally vulnerable to predatory raids by the competition? Is the interest rate fixed, or is it an adjustable one? Is there a balloon on the note?

These details aren't usually in the prospectus. They are things you have to negotiate with the seller, or sometimes with a third party lender. As I keep stressing every few pages, look beyond the surface! It may be possible the asking price that seems out of your reach can be twisted around to accommodate your budget. Keep these other factors in mind as you crunch numbers.

To answer most of the money questions about the sales price itself, you'll need three sets of figures. The seller has provided you with his. You'll need two of your own. One is the best estimate of what you think the various assets are really worth as they sit. The other is your estimate of what the total cost is going to be to put you in place.

That last statement could stand some explaining. Here's an example to illustrate the concept of the difference between the seller's price, your offering price, and your ultimate cost.

That chair in operatory number 2 is listed in the seller's inventory at $1,000. It's functional, but the upholstery's badly stained and there's a small rip or two in the fabric. As far as you're concerned it's only worth $500. You further estimate there'll be an additional cost to you almost immediately of $750 to get it reworked. (That's part of the positive image you figure you'll have to project to patients in order to retain them.)

The $500.00 figure is a definite bargaining chip to be placed on the table to help lower the total cost of the practice. The $750.00 refurbishing charge is an option you want to exercise after you buy, but is hardly something that interests the seller. As far as he's concerned you're buying "what is, as is." He has no overwhelming compulsion to underwrite your later improvements.

I should caution you to be careful with your wish list. Only include what you feel are absolute necessities. Curb any wild dreams of the perfect sparkling office for the moment. The truth is, if you have the wherewithal to indulge all your fancies, just forget all this negotiating foolishness and write the seller a check for whatever he wants! If you don't have that kind of loot, be practical.

As you can see, your task is to sit down with all that mass of data you've spent days or possibly weeks collecting and make sense out of it. This is not an exact science, but hopefully you can take it out of the crystal ball arena.

To simplify things, break the seller's appraisal into its various parts. The easiest to work with are the tangible assets, so let's get them out of the way first.

List all the major items on the inventory and what the seller thinks they're worth. Next to each item in a separate column, note what you, through your research, have determined the actual value is. Rarely will you find your total ends up greater than the seller's, but for the sake of being complete in offering a guide, you might set up a final separate worksheet and list the lesser of the two figures.

A suggestion. As you go through the list, make a note of why you considered your figure more reasonable than the seller's. This will help jog your memory when you do negotiate and will bolster your argument for a better deal. It goes without saying that you should keep mum about any items you thought were worth more than the seller's appraisal.

In the third column of your initial worksheet, put down the cost to repair or replace any equipment you're positive will go out if unattended to for a year or less. Add to that the cost of any equipment the office lacks that you feel is essential to your productivity.

Again the caution to be conservative. For example, as a general practitioner you might want to add a panoramic X-ray to the office. Realistically you can do without one for a long time and still deliver quality dentistry.

On the other hand, you might feel the lack of a hydrocolloid conditioner is critical. Not having one will compromise your talents and ability to deliver quality to your prospective patients. Leave off the X-ray and keep the hydrocolloid bath on the list.

Of course, if you're an oral surgeon, the panoramic view would undoubtedly be critical. If the office doesn't have this vital piece of equipment, put it down and marvel in the meantime how the seller managed to continue this long without.

When it comes to the miscellaneous items and supplies, you might as well accept the seller's figure. I suggest you add a few hundred dollars on your ultimate cost list to cover specific supplies and minor instruments you'll need immediately.

If the office space is leased, you'll probably find something called "leasehold improvements" in the appraisal. This tricky item is always open to question. There's no doubt the seller put a fair amount of money into someone else's property and would like very much to recoup some of it. This is fine only so long as you have firm written assurances you'll be able to take over the lease for enough time to make that expense worthwhile.

A bit of explanation. There is a fairly common practice in figuring leasehold improvements. A presumption is made the lease will run for five years beyond the date of the evaluation. The leasehold improvements are then depreciated over the period of time from their installation until the end of that five year lease or extension. However, if this would make the improvements more than 10 years old at the end of this term, then the balance is figured on the basis of a 10 year maximum. After that, only a minimal salvage value figure is acceptable.

First example. The seller leased the office five years ago and spent $20,000 to convert it to a dental office. The lease and guaranteed extensions will run for at least five more years. Using straight-line depreciation, the present value would then be in the neighborhood of $10,000.

Second example. The leasehold improvements are eight years old. Using the same figure of $20,000, the leasehold would only be worth $4,000 even though the lease may run for another five years.

A second, simpler method often favored is to assign an overall useful life to the improvements, then depreciate them on a straight-line basis. The term is usually from 12 to 15 years. I suggest you do the math both ways and see which comes out more favorable to you.

Normally this figure is something of a bargain unless it's a brand new office. It'd cost you far more to replace everything. Further, some appraisals deduct rather severely for wear and tear beyond what's apparent. This can lower the basic figure more than what's expected under the above rules.

You may also find a method of depreciation used other than straight line. There's declining balance, sum of the digits, and others. Have your accountant explain all of them to you. They'll apply to things you buy later even if they aren't applicable now. It'll also help you decide how to handle depreciation after you buy—something which might have an influence on your future expense sheet for tax purposes. This in turn could make a difference in the present affordability of the practice.

There are two hitches in the leasehold figure. Using the first method, you must ask yourself whether you will be able to extend the lease to cover that five year extension period under agreeable terms? If not, the leasehold improvements lose their value very rapidly.

The second potential problem is the rare case where the office is a disaster area needing paint, new floor coverings, serious plumbing attention, or other extensive or expensive work. Make your adjustments accordingly. Here you have a valid argument for knocking off something from the "goodwill" for deplorable conditions.

Sometimes leasehold improvements will be listed when the doctor owns the building and you'll be renting from him. It makes no difference. Treat this figure the same way you would if a third party was the lessor.

If you're buying the building at the same time you buy the practice, seriously consider balking at including this item as part of the practice purchase. It's definitely an item for negotiation. If you aren't careful, you might wind up paying double for the partitions. This is an area where you need to have talks with an experienced accountant and/or attorney. Uncle Sam's tax code can materially affect how this item is handled in this special situation.

In any office you look at, there will be equipment that has no earthly value as far as you're concerned. It may be a base for an old pump chair or a spanking new inlay casting machine. You may secretly want to tell the seller to move this junk out of your way.

Unfortunately, these items are often things the seller sets great store in and prizes highly. About all you can do is plan on selling them at a swap meet for what you can get. Don't let bits of unusable memorabilia stand in the way of an otherwise good deal.

When you've finished with the tangible assets, you'll regretfully turn to those not so tangible. I say regretfully, since the lake here is deep and murky. Much of the intangible asset value is a matter of personal, often biased, judgment.

For example, how much is a telephone number worth? Is the fact that the same receptionist sat in the same chair at the same window for nine years a sellable asset? It probably is, but how much is she worth? She might be a liability! Is a corporate logo worth anything? How about the neon sign with the blinking tooth which has become a community landmark? If marketable, how much are things like this really worth? More to the point, how much are they worth to you?

Some appraisals give a detailed base for the intangibles figure in a prospectus, others don't. Your job is a little easier if everything's spelled out for you. You can take the individual items and decide if they're reasonable or not.

A note. The assignment of goodwill figures to individual items has potential tax consequences. Large consequences. While this has little to do with the ultimate determination of the practice's worth, it does make a difference in negotiating a sale price. Find out beforehand what items have adverse tax consequences to both you and the seller. It'll be valuable when you do arrive at a final figure.

If the prospectus only gives a total figure without breakdown, you need to list the obvious intangible assets and assign a value to each. Alternatively, you can take a shortcut and use the gross revenue or net profit to estimate what the practice is worth in overall good will.

Traditionally, a figure of from four to eight month's gross receipts was often used as a yardstick measure of intangible goodwill. In taking this approach the evaluator generally starts with six months as a base and adds or subtracts subjectively for the stability, desirability, profitability, growth potential, and longevity of the practice.

An additional factor may be whether individual cost or income figures are growing, flat, or shrinking. A premium may also be placed on the location being in a growing, vital community where dental offices are snapped up in a hurry.

Several alternative schemes have been advanced in the past 10 years or so to try and remove the subjectivity from determining goodwill. They take various names, including cash stream, capitalization, excess capitalization, or excess income. All produce dandy little worksheets your banker will love and which you should have your accountant explain if you're so inclined. Whether one's more accurate than the next is anyone's guess.

The main purported advantage to these various approaches is they produce a bottom line which proponents claim allows for easy comparison of different practices. Without going into detail, there are shortcomings to all of these methods. The fair market value figure arrived at can be quite unrealistic when applied to any singe practice.

Some of these methods become extremely complicated. Some may include tangible assets in the figures. Some consider them separately. Some take the tax return depreciated value for equipment, some arbitrarily assign a 12 year life span to it, then knock off about 8 percent for every year it's been in service. Every wrinkle in this evaluation process has its proponents who advance great arguments for their method being the most accurate.

Though it's slightly off the subject, you, as a buyer, should *not* view any appraisal, no matter how professionally done, as an accurate determination of fair market value. Rather, think of it as an appraised value that looks good on a financial statement and a "fattener" for a loan package. The fact is, dental practices seldom sell for as much as their appraised value. Medical practices, on the other hand, often sell at a premium.

So much for fair market value accuracy. Back to your problems.

A more useful approach which has fallen into some disrepute is to use a year's net profit as a fair determination of goodwill. This may also be adjusted according to any of the factors listed above.

Why is this method better for you? Consider for a moment two practices that gross $400,000. In one, the net is $150,000. The other net is only $75,000. I think you'll agree the first is more valuable to you as a buyer than the second, even though technically they'd probably be valued equally if judged solely by the gross. The alternative methods will also provide some false results, especially those that do not list tangible assets separately.

I think you'll agree the low-net office may have more potential for improving profitability, but you're not really too wise to buy into an untried potential net growth without demanding a deep discount. There'd be no margin for error on the down side if you're wrong.

*Deciding If A Practice Is Reasonably Priced*

Another method useful in special cases is to assign a dollar value to each patient record. This could be a two-or three-year patient base as discussed earlier, or a declining scale depending on how current each record is, or even on how soon a patient comes back into the office for treatment.

You might find this type of appraisal useful in a practice that's heavily into HMO managed care. Here, the actual annual worth of each patient is known. Their worth would then be in inverse proportion to the utilization rate of the group as a whole.

That is, if half the patients come in for treatment each year, the factor would be 50 percent. A further adjustment could be made for the average treatment each patient received. The best use of an exercise of this sort would be to assess the effect on the practice's worth if part of the contracts the office has are not transferable.

A further use of this novel alternative is in the case of the "dead" practice—one which has been closed for an extended period. The goodwill in this situation is minimal to non-existent. Even so, there may be a modest patient base available to be tapped.

Offering the selling party a fixed sum for each patient actually recaptured over an agreed upon time span can have advantages to both parties. The seller has a reasonable chance to recoup more of the potential value of the practice, while the buyer doesn't buy anything that isn't really there. Such an arrangement may also allow the buyer to gain more favorable terms for the rest of the assets.

You may find a projection page somewhere in the prospectus. It may be used as an argument for an increased valuation. Ignore it in your deliberations. Only a very young practice can reasonably expect to grow on a compounded basis over the next three, five, or 10 years. As mentioned elsewhere, this popularly included figure is most likely thrown in primarily as a sales tool. It's also a delightful adjunct to your loan package at the bank.

Why should you ignore it? There may be a bit of validity to a claim that a starting practice has that sort of potential growth. Most practices continue to expand up until the age of five to seven years, but don't count on it! Many practices hit their effective peak very rapidly.

How do you tell when the limits are reached? If it appears the appointment book in that infant practice is pretty full, the potential for significant expansion may be limited unless an associate is added or other radical changes are made. If the appraiser included a figure for potential expansion in his estimate, cross it out immediately. You're buying "what is, as is," not "what is, what might be."

This is not to say you shouldn't privately take the possibility of growth potential lightly in your deliberations. You may see tremendous opportunities for improvement in the practice, but don't let it sway you into jumping in blindly. There may be a good reason the seller hasn't opted for these changes himself.

Conversely, you may spot things that will inhibit your expanding the practice or even maintaining it at the current level. For example, the seller may be putting in 60 hours a week— living, breathing, and occasionally sleeping the practice. His reason for selling may be burnout. You know you're not about to follow in those footsteps, thus making the continued present production figures improbable.

Not all cases are this extreme. Still, some practices have hidden traps you need to look for. I'll cite two more quick examples. One was a most reasonably priced office with real paper potential for growth. The only hitch was, unless you belonged to a particular local religious sect, you didn't stand a church-specific prayer of making a living. Unless a buyer wanted to convert, the actual value of the practice was probably limited to not much more than the tangible assets.

The same is true of two small towns I know of. Each was originally settled and still populated almost exclusively by a distinct ethnic group. Unless you also happened to have the proper surname and/or a working knowledge of the language imported from the old country, you'd be well advised to pass on by. This condition may also be found in major cities where recent immigrants have congregated together for mutual support.

On the bright side, if you *do* fit the requirements, you may have a unique opportunity waiting for you. This brings up a touchy philosophical point. If the idea of trading on your skin color, the slant of an eye, your mother's unpronounceable maiden name, or the bit of foreign language you picked up while in the service is abhorrent to you, stop a moment and reflect.

These groups are entitled to dental services just as much as anyone else. If your appearance, ancestry, or linguistic skill makes it more comfortable for a potential patient, why not be willing to accommodate a real need?

Other factors you may want to consider when arriving at your goodwill figure include the age of not only the practice, but that of the doctor and the patients. It's generally true that the patient pool of an older dentist tends to be older, too. Ask yourself very seriously if you have enough in common with the patients to treat them without making them feel you're too young, or they're too old for your serious consideration.

I can assure you from personal early experience in private practice, it does little for your confidence level to have a grizzled patient look you up and down and blurt, "Sonny, I don't think you're old enough to know *how* to make a bridge!"

Don't forget the attitude and stability of the staff. Of importance in assessing both the staff and staff/patient interaction are the following: the attitude of the staff concerning the type of clientele served, the mix of services delivered, the amount and percentage of partial payment as a result of alternative delivery agreements, the training and skill levels of the staff, the personality traits individually and collectively, the appearance, the age mix, and more. You'll undoubtedly think of other factors as you go along.

Without running afoul of governmental edicts regarding age discrimination, I should point out that in some practices the presence of a "grandmother" type can be beneficial. They can often help bridge the generation gap between a younger doctor and an aging patient pool.

Other factors to be considered in assessing goodwill include the transferability of alternative treatment agreements, gross/net ratio, large swings in production and gross income from year to year, and unfavorable production/collection ratios. All practices have negative factors, but too many should be a warning sign to lower the final goodwill figure.

A note. If there are large swings in overhead figures from year to year, check out at least four years, possibly five, to see if the doctor is stacking expenses and income for tax purposes. If this is the case, try re-allocating figures to their proper year to arrive at a more accurate picture.

One final item to consider is the possibility of hidden liabilities. This is something the seller may not be aware of himself. I refer to deferred costs that will be transferred to you when you buy the practice. One example mentioned earlier is the responsibility for unemployment taxes that the seller has incurred as a result of unjustly firing an unsatisfactory employee. The office may have acquired a horrible unemployment insurance rating as a result.

Unfair as it may seem, you could have this liability and rating passed on to you when you purchase the practice. By all means, ask the seller if any such clouds are hanging over the practice. It may save you a continuing unpleasant and expensive surprise months or even years after you've settled in.

A pitfall of purchasing a corporation is that the corporation may not actually own much. Many doctors use the corporate shield to transfer assets to their family to gain favorable tax treatment. You may assume you're buying assets you'll end up having to lease later on!

You should consult with both an accountant and an attorney about the ramifications of buying stock in the seller's corporation instead of buying the practice assets outright. There are significant tax consequences in addition to other potential hidden hazards. You might want to alter your figures downward in such a case.

Once you've completed your three lists, it's time to make sense out of them. To do so, you need just one more set of figures.

The assumption here is you're going to have to finance a good part of the purchase price. Whether you're borrowing the money from a third party lender, the seller, or some combination of both is immaterial. Borrowed money obviously has to be repaid out of the activity of the practice. The big question then becomes whether the practice realistically will support both you and the debt?

This can be a trick question. There are a number of variables to consider and a number of assumptions you may have to make in order to arrive at a reasonable answer. Many can't be reduced to hard numbers on a page at this point, but should be allowed for. This statement should become self-explanatory as we go along, so don't throw up your hands just yet. It's not quite time for your crystal ball.

For now, let's deal with hard facts. If you find any of the following conditions lie outside your comfort zone or financial reach, you might be well advised to back off.

If you've gone this far in your analysis, you've undoubtedly found out what you'll have to have in the way of a down payment. To this, add closing costs.

Yes, there will be closing costs. Significant closing costs. Include attorney fees, accountant fees, other consultant fees, filing fees, and maybe pro-rated tax liabilities. It isn't uncommon for these to be several thousand dollars, maybe as much as $10,000 or more, depending on the conditions of the sale and the extent to which you've turned to other professionals for advice.

On top of this you'll need additional money to cover those items in the tangible asset list you've prepared. You should also plan on putting adequate money in a reserve account for those rough months when patients avoid your door in substantial numbers.

Many practices are surprisingly seasonal. Almost all practices see a big slump at Christmas. Tax time will invariably slow the cash flow. I'd advise being a bit generous in your estimate of this dry weather reserve.

How much of a reserve should you maintain? Another tough question. A prudent figure might be to allow for as much as three to six months of basic office overhead plus minimal living expenses. You may want to peruse the chapter on fees for a discussion of what's true overhead.

Hopefully you won't need a dime, but it's comforting to have it in reserve, just in case. You'll either have to have this in savings or arrange for a line of credit at your bank. Your ulcer will thank you for this foresight.

Now you have a mass of processed data. What do you do with it? Let's turn to the financing part of your deliberations. If you're dealing with a commercial lender, you should have a pretty good idea of how much you can borrow even at this stage.

Add your down payment to this amount. If you must borrow to cover either closing costs or other expenses discussed above, subtract them from this figure. This will tell you what you can afford to pay for the practice. You must negotiate down to, or below, this figure or walk away.

Your next test will be the continuing expenses you're looking at. You know what it costs the seller to run the office every month and you should have snooped deeply enough to see what economies are available.

I'd suggest you use the larger of the two figures. Better to allow for a bit of error than to find yourself caught short a few months down the line. If your estimate of expenses is greater than those of the current owner, definitely use that figure.

Add to this the monthly mortgage payment you're facing when you buy the practice, plus any additional continuing expenses you foresee that the seller doesn't have. An example might be life insurance called for by many mortgage outfits. If the seller is financing, he may want this security, too.

Though few sellers or bankers want it, the inclusion of a disability insurance package is something you should seriously consider. Nobody ever plans on being sick or getting hurt, but it happens. If you should need this security blanket down the line, you'll be mighty glad you opted for it.

If the deal is to be owner financed, you should have a good idea of the length of time he's going to allow for repayment and the interest rate he wants. Any bank can furnish you with an amortization schedule, or your handy calculator or computer may be equipped to work it out for you in a couple of minutes. Either way, add the monthly payment to the basic overhead.

Hold on to this figure and turn to the average monthly gross receipts for the practice. Discount them a minimum of 10 percent, or preferably 20 percent. The reason for a discount? There's no guarantee you'll be as productive as the seller initially. You may lose a few patients simply because you aren't Dr. X, the seller.

A warning. The mere fact you see potential for increasing efficiency or production doesn't necessarily mean an automatic improvement in either the gross or net of the practice. It takes time. Better be unnecessarily prepared for the worst case scenario than to be caught unaware.

Next, subtract your projected liabilities from your adjusted gross figure. Unless you can live and pay all your personal bills in a timely fashion on the remaining amount, you may well be heading for trouble.

If you find you're marginal and want to cut yourself a little extra slack, look back at the seller's goodwill calculations. In them you may find a section which details accounts receivable. There are two problems associated with buying this most dubious asset.

First, there's no way that figure will remain static for more than a week in a going office. Second, you have no earthly conception of how collectable those accounts really are.

The collection percentages assigned to the older accounts reflecting their collectability may bear no relationship whatsoever to reality. You'll probably find that with the seller gone, they become much more difficult to collect.

Try asking the seller to take them off the table and merely give you a small percentage for collecting them for him. If he's agreeable, offer to do the paper work for something like 10 percent of actual collections. Get in writing what's to be turned over to an outside agency for servicing if it comes to that. Better still, suggest he take copies of those records with him and fill in some idle hours writing past due notes!

For what it's worth, the bigger the cushion you have between income and expenses, the better you'll sleep at night. If, for example, your projection of the consequences of a 20 percent drop in the gross leaves no room for emergencies, you may be in trouble. If the break-even point is 90 percent of current gross, you have a serious potential problem if you buy.

Incidentally, your accountant may be able to do all this figuring for you if you ask him for a pro-forma. His computer can spit out results in minutes and allow you to play with variable scenarios regarding length of time of your mortgage, various possible interest rates, altering the down payment, overhead items, gross receipts, and more.

You may find this actuarially-accepted formal method of information collation to be of great help with a loan officer. It may prove equally helpful in your negotiations with the seller. If nothing else, it can keep you from jumping in the deep end of the money pool without knowing what's under the water.

There are a number of special situations which will alter the standard approach to your deciding what that practice is worth to you. In no particular order, they are: an associate buying into a practice, the purchase of a partial interest in a group practice, the seller wishing to remain active in the practice as either a part- or full-time associate, the escalating buyout where the buyer assumes an ever larger share of the practice in incremental steps, buying out a partner in a group practice, buying into a group practice as a partner without initially working as an associate, and the "fire sale."

I suspect that as the management of dental practices becomes more convoluted and specially designed practice arrangements become more in demand, this list will grow.

The central difficulty associated with most of these special cases is determining a fair price for the asset the buyer is acquiring. For example, if an associate buys into a practice after working for the seller for several years, should the selling price be based on the assets at the time the associate first comes on board? Should it be determined as of the date the sale is agreed upon? Or somewhere in between?

Here's the rub. If the sale is based on the worth of the practice at the time the associate first starts, it's obvious he's buying into a practice that's worth more than it was when he started. How much of that growth is attributable to him is the issue.

Conversely, if the price reflects the results of his labor as figured on the later date, he's in essence paying the seller a premium for the effort the hapless associate put into the practice. Hopefully there was an initial agreement when the associate was hired. If not, a big bunch of negotiating's going to take place!

Why? Obviously it's undisputed the practice is undoubtedly worth more at the time it's offered for sale to an outside buyer than it would've been before the addition of the associate. Assuredly the seller should be compensated in some measure for the risk he took when hiring an associate. He may have had additional expenses back then, too. Likewise, the associate shouldn't be penalized for working his brains out to build the practice and develop his own following.

To further complicate matters, negotiations must be done with the best grade kid gloves available if the seller is remaining in the practice in any capacity. If either party feels they've been treated shabbily, the harmonious relationship of the two, and thus the practice's future earnings, will potentially suffer.

One of the many possible problems that can arise is illustrated by the difficulty in determining future incremental purchases leading to a full partnership. One sticky spot is the distribution of future earnings above and beyond a set compensation for each party's production or attendance in the practice.

For example, a seller may work down to only showing up one day a week, and then spending most of that time doing nothing. However, the mere fact his name's still on the door may produce a disproportionate number of patients for the practice. That they must be transferred to another practitioner doesn't diminish his basic value to the outfit. He's obviously worth more than just his production would indicate, but how much? How do you measure it?

In the situation where a buyer is investing in a group practice or even in a two-person partnership, the question of who's in control routinely arises. Restrictions imposed by the controlling doctor may chafe badly in a short time, leading to dissatisfaction and dissension. The buyer may also find getting into an ultimately unsatisfactory arrangement was much easier than getting out. Unfortunately this is not always spelled out in the sales agreement.

As noted earlier, buying into a corporation presents the potential for some tax headaches, at least under the tax structure as it exists at the time this is being written. Also, it's much easier for liabilities to be buried under the corporate foundation. Other knotty problems may crop up in or after such a stock transfer. Whether you're buying a bit of the corporation or the whole thing, spend extra time with your attorney and accountant.

When dealing with these special situations, you'd be well advised to call upon the services of an experienced management consultant who's well versed in this area. He won't come cheap, but he'll pay for himself in a hurry. This is *not* the place for a do-it-yourself project! It may not be necessary for the consultant to conduct all the negotiations, but his expertise will be invaluable in helping you work out an arrangement you can live with comfortably.

One other situation may arise to trap the unwary. On occasion the seller will be offering a package deal of an office building and a practice. You may find the figures intermingled in the financial material you're given. Break the building and the practice apart as much as possible and, if you're interested in purchasing both, negotiate for each separately.

Above all, don't allow the practice and the building to be lumped into one package for financing purposes. Have your attorney explain the bottomless pit you could fall into under such an arrangement. In case you haven't spotted one obvious problem yourself, try explaining to yourself why you'd want to sign a document allowing the seller to come back in and take everything back

10 to 20 years later just because you somehow missed a payment while taking that six-week European luxury tour!

On the same subject, you may discover that if you're leasing the building from the seller, the lease is tied into the practice sale under a similar arrangement. This isn't too much of a burden if your payment schedule doesn't stretch out too far. It does offer the seller a bit of extra security. Usually this doesn't create a hardship for the buyer unless he has plans to move the practice in a couple of years. That could be a real problem. So, as with all bits of paper, know what you're signing.

The emergency sale does create some interesting situations. The biggest one is determining what, if any, goodwill is available. Some practices offered are on the market due to ill health or death of the doctor. Remember that a practice's worth deteriorates when the doors are closed for any extended period of time.

Deterioration may have been slowed or accelerated by the presence of a dentist being hired to take care of routine work in the office. Months undoubtedly will have elapsed from the time the office was closed until you come on the scene.

By all means, deeply discount the worth of the goodwill in this situation. It doesn't matter that you feel sorry for the doctor who's been stricken, or have sympathy for a survivor in the case of death. That practice is not worth what it was when the doctor was going full tilt. It isn't even worth what it was when the ad was placed.

Not only does the time lapse merely mean that patients have drifted away. In all probability only one or two of the staff are still on the scene to provide a bit of continuity for the patients who ultimately remain. The longer the office has been closed, or open without the owner's driving force, the more you should discount.

There's no formula available to make this discount easy to figure. Each situation is different. You must use your own judgment here. Just be aware you're looking at a wounded practice and adjust your forecast of what's left accordingly.

In making that adjustment, remember you're not going to be in that office immediately. Factor in the time lapse that's bound to occur even after you've struck a preliminary deal. It'll require several months to get all the paperwork taken care of. Consider seriously the alternative of buying the tangible assets and using the method described previously of striking a bargain based on the number of patients who end up returning.

Though it's not a guidepost, it used to be said that a practice closed for more than six months had nothing more than salvage value. The only exception to this might be the rare case where the seller is unable to practice, but is still in a position to exert a true positive influence on his former patients. Even then, proceed with caution.

If it's possible for you to actually go to work before the final contracts are signed, by all means do so. This will naturally depend on your own availability and the proximity of the practice to your present location. Even a part-time exposure to the remaining patients will be to your benefit.

As you can plainly see, merely adding up the numbers is not always enough. The seller may unconsciously attach a premium for his love of the profession and his participation in that office. You may likewise attach a premium you're willing to pay for the privilege of getting into your own practice—or into that particular practice. There can also be an unwarranted premium in the asking price inserted by a broker to fatten his commission.

There's nothing wrong with either of the principals falling in love with a particular private practice. It's probably a darned good thing to have that approach when you do finally settle in. Please, don't let it override whatever good judgment you have when assessing your chances for success in that situation.

A final note. If you've collected and gone through all the figures and facts outlined above and have digested them, you deserve a night out before you proceed to the next phase of purchase—the negotiation.

# Chapter 13

# Financing

Since we've arrived at the negotiation stage of our deliberations, perhaps now would be as good a time as any to detour from the main objective long enough to make a few observations about financing. Some of the items have been touched on in earlier discussions, but it won't hurt to repeat them in the context of putting together a finance package.

There was a time when almost any professional could walk into a bank, spend 10 minutes telling someone how much he/she needed, sign a personal note and be gone with large amounts of cash. That came to an abrupt halt in the 1980s.

At one low point, even a well-established practitioner had to beg and plead for anything more than pocket change. At the present time the banking mood has moved back toward a more reasonable spot on the financial dial, but it's far from automatic that a loan will be forthcoming for funds to buy or start a practice. Things like credit rating, positive cash flow, net asset value, and other positive attributes are required for being looked on favorably. In short, we dentists are now treated just like every other small business owner when we need money. We've become a commercial entity, individually and as a profession.

So, unless you're the rare exception, you'll need more money than you have if you intend to open your own office, buy out an existing practice, or become a full fledged member of a group or partnership. That means the terms and condition of any note you sign will materially affect your ability to pay your basic obligation from practice income. It will also materially affect the amount you can afford to spend initially.

Many an unwary neophyte, and unhappily, some experienced hands, have been burned badly by not knowing just what the fine print in their loan agreement ties them to. You may end up having to accept some of the following less than desirable options, but you should be aware of their implications. If you have any niggling doubts about what all those "whereas" things on page 32 of your note mean, get immediate help translating them to real English! Before you sign!

A balloon note may be offered as a way of reducing your monthly payments. The note is usually figured on the basis of up to a 30-year payback, but the unpaid balance is due in a shorter period of time, usually two to five years. At that point the note must either be renegotiated or the borrower must come up with a big chunk of change. Renegotiation may well mean accepting larger payments or an increased interest rate. It's also conceivable the lender won't refinance, leaving you out in the drifting snow.

There's another nasty little price connected to the string on the balloon. That's the cost of renewing the little jewel. The costs you incurred initially in fees may be repeated every time you have to renew the note. Sometimes these run into four figures and can be a shocker if you're not prepared. Your kindly banker, if he likes you, may offer to tack them onto the principal, thus leaving you paying interest on them as well as the note balance you have to bargain for.

The second bottomless pit is the floating mortgage rate, or "prime, plus." Far too many otherwise sound businesses went under the hammer some years ago when the effective interest rate planned on suddenly went orbital, rising to as much as 25 percent. When combined with the worst features of the balloon note, "prime, plus" can produce a total disaster.

Another version of this is when you're asked to make a fixed payment on the principal, plus whatever interest has accrued. With this type of arrangement you're not in trouble unless the floating interest rate goes up a couple of notches. Then you have to come up with a significantly larger payment every month. This can put a real crimp in your food budget if you're not sitting on something of a cushion.

Negative financing is a little hinged trap that offers the illusory advantage of paying a fixed amount that's less than the true payment should be for the first part of the note's lifetime. The unpaid portion is quietly added to the principal, creating a larger debt than originally contracted for. When the time comes to actually reduce the principal, there can be an outsized bolt of reality lightning.

*Financing*

When this bit of retail jewelry is combined with an adjustable rate, you'd be well advised to seek a part time job in one of the local fast food eateries to supplement your income. Only the good Lord can help if you have several of these financing tricks dumped on you and things go sour in the general economy.

You might also be offered the option of a variation of this in which no payment at all is made for a number of months "to let you get your feet on the ground." It's great on the surface, but may put you in a bind when you wake up and find you owe a bigger note than you thought you would, because no one bothered to tell you the interest meter was ticking merrily away.

There are other convoluted twists to these common practices too numerous to mention. I shall again issue the caution of consulting someone who can explain these little winding financial paths to you, one who doesn't stand to make a buck out of the resulting agreement.

Second mortgages have come into vogue in the last few years and are touted by some management advisors as a creative way to place you into a practice you otherwise couldn't afford.

In a second mortgage financing deal, you arrange a loan from a commercial lending institution for the amount of the practice that can be secured by tangible assets. This allows you to pay off all the closing costs and fees surrounding the purchase. The balance is used as a down payment to the seller. The seller then takes a second mortgage on the remainder, roughly the amount of the intangible assets, plus whatever you've had to fork over to the other people who have their hands out.

The catch here is that in the event of a default on the buyer's part, the poor guy holding a second mortgage may have to pay off the first mortgage in order to resume control of the practice. If he doesn't, then he loses everything except that small down payment and whatever he received in payments in the meantime.

I'm sure you can appreciate the added risk the second mortgage holder has. Naturally, he's going to want a significantly larger interest rate as a reward for taking this risk. This may not sound too bad until you figure that the general rule at the moment on second mortgages is to charge at least another four percentage points above what the holder of the first mortgage charges.

Getting complicated? Here's an example. Suppose the bank's prime rate is 8 percent. Since the buyer's coming into this deal with little or no cash up front, the bank thinks it's a bit of a risk. There's potential, and the loan's secured, but there's still a risk. So, they add on three points to prime as the interest rate.

The seller, knowing he's personally able to borrow at prime plus one percent, feels he's taking a bigger-than-average risk because the bank views the buyer that way. So, Dr. Seller adds on another five percent over what the bank charges. You can do the math in your head—16 percent. You can get a better deal on a credit card if you shop around. If they both come up with an adjustable rate, the buyer could end up with a payment he can only see with a telescope.

Another thing to remember when doing your homework is to take into account that your loan will be classified as a commercial one. You won't get that lovely 30 year pay-back period you're offered when you buy a cute little two-bedroom starter home. This holds true also when you buy the building the practice is housed in. For loans like these, 10 years is routinely the outside maximum time, and less is usually preferred.

One or two general notes on obtaining advantageous financing. First and foremost, make sure your personal credit record is as clean as it can be. Do this as soon as you begin to think about buying a practice or setting up on your own. Starting even sooner won't hurt.

To do this, contact all of the major credit bureaus and request a copy of your credit history. Go over it carefully to see if there are any errors, and have these corrected immediately. If there are bad spots that aren't errors, list the reasons for any late or missed payments on anything you borrowed money for. Request that these explanations be placed in your file.

For example, maybe you were late on a car payment because you or your spouse were sick and couldn't work. Or, you were in the service, were transferred, and your pay records were temporarily lost so you didn't have funds to make the payment. Lenders do understand things like this and are willing to overlook an occasional lapse. What they don't like is seeing an habitual sloppy attitude toward debt.

When you have a clean credit sheet, start making arrangements for financing as soon in the process of setting up shop as possible. Visit several banks to determine how receptive they might be to your idea of becoming a borrower. Go armed with that trusty financial statement and a copy of your credit history.

If you've dealt with a loan officer before, he's the one to see. If you're heading for a new community, ask your present banker for a recommendation as to your trustworthiness. If there's a branch of the same bank you're dealing with now, suggest the new banker call a specific someone in your present location for additional information.

While you won't get a loan commitment at this early date, a good loan

*Financing*

officer can tell you roughly what your chances will be of obtaining financing, give you an idea of the upper limits of your general borrowing capacity, and generally explain the terms. Having this information will make your negotiating with a potential seller a lot more pleasant.

What will a loan officer want to see at this initial visit? He'll probably ask for very little. Nevertheless, go prepared. Already mentioned were the financial statement, which should reflect your net worth, and your credit history. Add to this a breakdown of your current and probable future personal expenses— things like student loan payments, car payments, house payments, general living expenses including recurring credit card charges, taxes, personal insurance, and the like. It won't hurt to have specific details of your personal expenses broken into various categories. Your tax returns for a couple of years will be needed down the line, so throw them in the file now.

If you're married, include your spouse's income and job-related expenses. Child care, additional clothing requirements, and unreimbursed travel expense are examples. If you're relocating, they'll want to know what her job opportunities are in the new community.

Chances are good your soulmate will be asked to sign the note and the bank wants to know if, and to what extent, your spouse can take on the burden— or at least a part of your debt. Bankers in general have a distinct aversion to sharing your suffering if something nasty happens to you.

In that regard, it won't hurt to have a bit of proof of insurability. According to the local branch manager of a large regional bank, few professionals think of having a decent disability policy in their files. If you're not currently carrying one, get one that allows you to increase the limits automatically to cover the additional expense of the loan. Because so few professionals bother with this insurance, this little touch will show a sense of responsibility not normally found.

Another nice bit of information a banker likes is a comparative statement of an increase in your personal net worth. Bankers like people who are able to save money. It indicates a responsible attitude toward finances. Again, the prevailing attitude of doctors of all ilk is to take whatever cash flow they may have and spend it down to the last penny. Only professional athletes can outdo us in this area.

One pertinent question you need to ask at this initial meeting is what additional information you'll have to come up with when you do make formal application for a specific loan. At that time you're going to be rushed, harried, and anxious. You'll resent every minute you have to spend digging out what seem like useless bits of trivia to satisfy some distant loan committee.

I'll guarantee they'll come back for more paperwork no matter how complete your presentation is, but the fewer times you have to drop everything and go chasing after "just one more" figure, the happier you'll be. To get you started, here are some of the basic things you'll need:

1. The entire package of information provided by a seller. This should include the practice valuation, including an equipment breakdown and appraisal, three years of business tax returns provided by the seller, any projections or pro-forma statements generated by the seller, the original asking price if it's not the same as the appraisal, and any other documents pertinent to the potential sale.

2. Obviously, you'll need your own projections of any changes in practice status after you take over or buy in, your "worst case scenario" pro-forma backing your claim you won't have to declare bankruptcy in six months, a list of additional expenses you'll have as a result of being in the practice, an outline of terms you think you can live with, and/or a statement of how you would like to pay back whatever you borrow.

3. You should also include a short statement of what portion of your own funds are going into this venture and what you intend to hold in reserve as a contingency for adverse conditions that may arise. The more of your own money you're willing to risk, the better your chances of obtaining a loan.

If you happen to have enough for a sizeable down payment, but for some reason, such as tax advantages, you don't want to put it directly on the table, consider buying a certificate of deposit from the bank and pledging it as a guarantee against the note.

4. If you feel any of this material needs explaining, put it in writing and attach it to the appropriate sheet of paper. Even though you've presented your case convincingly orally, a loan committee has no way of knowing that what the loan officer tells them is exactly what you said. Make things easy for them, too.

*Financing*

5. Not always required at this stage (but helpful) would be a copy of an initial escrow agreement outlining the general terms of the sale. This should include things like guarantee of lease transfer, statements from any applicable alternative providers indicating that you are welcome to continue that relationship without interruption on the same terms as the seller. A list of projected closing costs and fees you will owe to your consultants and advisors should be considered at this point.

6. A statement of acknowledgment from anyone who's offering to cosign your note along with their credit and financial details. This is all in addition to the financial data you offered initially on your first visit to the lender.

7. If you're striking out on your own, your file won't be as thick. To your personal history and that of your spouse, add the cost of the equipment you intend to buy, projected overhead analyses, lease agreements, and any HMO or PPO agreements which will generate immediate cash flow. A statement as to why you think the location you've selected is a good one that offers an opportunity not now being exploited is a good selling point.

This volume of material may seem like overkill to you, but to the lender it shows you've done some thinking about what you're getting into. Lending money is not a finite science. Lenders like to have more assurance than your word and good honest looks on which to base their gut feelings about lending you large sums of money. Make it as easy as possible for them to approve you.

To put it bluntly, when they're forking out for something as nebulous as "goodwill" or "potential," they're essentially making a personal loan. Do everything you can to make them feel good about you.

Less traumatic is the situation where a seller is financing your purchase. To begin with, the seller is acutely aware of what you're buying. He's fully aware of the probabilities of practice expansion. The chances are he's more interested in your professional ability to pay him than your past credit history. He'll tend to concentrate on your technical dental skills and consider your financial state only in passing.

Here, you probably won't need all that much paper. A statement of financial worth, your credit report, and an outline of any side income you or your spouse may have may be all that's required.

Even this minimal information may not be necessary if you've worked in the practice for a time as an associate, but don't count on it. Each circumstance and situation is different. The seller may have advisors who'd like to see figures before telling him how to structure any sales contract.

Where do you go if both the friendly bank you've been dealing with and the seller turn down your loan request? Don't despair completely. By all means, check with other banks or savings and loan outfits. They don't all use the same loan committee. More than one doctor has had to beat several doors down to find one that's cooperative.

If you're still turned down, there are at least three other sources you could try to tap. The first is the loan program sponsored by the ADA. A phone call will obtain particulars. The second is the Small Business Administration. I'll warn you, you're in for a great deal of frustrating red tape, but there is money available. Be prepared for that aforementioned frustration and delays! Be prepared to negotiate for the eventual release of any future grandchildren from involuntary servitude. You and the intervening generation will be tied up forever, but it's possible to free those future tykes if you're lucky. This method of financing is a true test of how desperately you wish to enter private practice!

The time factor in obtaining one of these loans is also a deterrent, but there is money there, and if you're dogged enough, you may latch on to some of it.

The third source may be the practice broker who's handling the sale. He may have contacts you aren't aware of that can assist you. The interest rate may not be as favorable as through a bank, but if the numbers are reasonably favorable, it may be your answer.

In special situations there is a fourth place to try. In some communities that qualify as depressed areas, there may be little known governmental programs designed to help businesses of all types locate there. While this would involve moving the office you're buying, it's just possible the practice you're looking at may sit right next to one of these eligible communities. If the move is only a couple of blocks, it might be worth looking into. Just remember the disadvantages listed elsewhere about moving an office when you buy it.

If you're starting from scratch in one of these so-called depressed areas, you might even be eligible for an outright grant. The place to start is city hall with the city manager's office. The way these programs are designed, there's the possibility the city may also qualify for a grant based on your participation. In this case, everybody in officialdom will turn Olympic cartwheels to assist you with the paper blizzard. However, don't expect miracles overnight. These

*Financing*

grants take a lot of time to process!

I might point out that in small towns, city hall may not be aware of some of these programs. You may have to do some research yourself to point the way to them. Having made the ultimate mistake of serving one term as an alderman in a wayside hamlet, I'll testify there are many federal programs that are unknown unless you dig around in the governmental back yard. If you dig deeply and long enough, it's amazing what you'll find.

For the beginner who's not had a great deal of time to set aside a backlog of cash, leasing equipment may be an option. Leased equipment doesn't show up on a balance sheet or a net worth statement. This may enable someone with limited borrowing power to scrounge up enough money to convert that empty office space into a dental office.

This option should be used cautiously, since it usually creates a larger short-term obligation that must be met monthly. If you opt for this solution to your front-money problem, watch out you don't create a mountain of monthly bills that'll keep you on the edge of insolvency.

Leasing can open up one other inventive way of creating cash out of thin air for a practice purchase. That's the variation of straightforward equipment leasing called the sale/lease-back. When used prudently it can be a useful tool for the cash-starved beginner buying a practice.

It works something like this. At the time of transfer of title to the tangible assets during a practice sale, the major equipment is sold to, then immediately leased back from the leasing company. The proceeds can then be applied to the down payment, or applied to other closing costs the buyer incurred.

If you try this trick, be sure you have clear title to the equipment. Be very, very sure you aren't selling mortgaged equipment! Your lawyer will be happy to explain the length of jail time being sloppy with this option can lead to.

A final thought on this whole subject. The most expert advice you can receive on imaginative financing is in the mind of a good banker who's experienced in commercial lending. It's even better if he's made a few loans for the same purpose you're after. Pick his brains. This is one place where you can get free advice. Ask for it.

# Chapter 14

# Notes On Negotiating The Purchase

This will be a fairly short chapter and is only given its own special heading since there doesn't seem to be another place to fit the following bits of advice. As the art of negotiation is a vast subject well covered in both popular and specialized texts and is much too broad to outline here, only a few general observations will be made. I'd urge you to review some of the preceding material where negotiation is referred to in the context of why you're doing other investigations. It'll avoid needless repetition and give you a better overall picture of what you're heading into.

You have no urgent reason to become a professional in this field, nor does the seller. Unless you suspect your natural skill at insisting on getting what's important to you or have no resolve or will to stick to your cannons, you probably won't need outside help in finalizing your agreement. That is, provided you've done your homework.

There's only one excuse for negotiation. That is to arrive at a meeting of minds between a willing seller and serious buyer. The thing to remember is, you both have ideas about the structure and financial details of your agreement. They aren't identical.

What the seller generally wants is as much money as he can milk out of the practice. What you want is as little debt or investment as possible. You have the additional interest in seeing the debt you assume will be manageable. That is, the practice will pay for the burden you're assuming, plus a decent living in the meantime.

If you don't feel comfortable handling a face-to-face confrontation, you have two choices. The first is to hire someone to speak for you. This can be your attorney, your accountant, or a broker or other agent you hire who's familiar with the purchase of dental practices.

The other method is to simply present the seller with a detailed written offer. If you're negotiating long distance, this may be your best bet. The seller can then mull over what you've offered and either accept, decline, or make a counter proposal. If you choose this method, don't outline any reasons for your offer. Save them for whatever objections the seller may raise.

Choose whichever method you feel will be most effective to protect your interests during this critical phase of dealing with the seller. However, before you do either, take your facts and figures to either an accountant who is familiar with the tax law covering such a sale or to an attorney who is well versed in these matters.

As mentioned elsewhere, Uncle Sam has a great deal to say about your purchase, both from your view and that of the seller. In many states with income taxes, the whammy is doubled. Where cities have adopted income taxes, there's additional compounding of any error that occurs.

The way the assets are categorized will have a tremendous influence on the tax bite the seller is liable for immediately. While you may feel sorry for the guy, be aware that if the deal is written to maximize his tax advantages, it can, and generally does, adversely reflect on your annual bill for years to come.

For this reason, I'd advise that you have a written proposal laid out before you talk to the seller. In this document, outline precisely what you want for the amount you're willing to fork over. Simply telling the seller you'll give him X dollars for his practice isn't enough. Be specific not only about what you're willing to pay and how long you'll take to pay it, but how the money he gets is allocated in the contract.

I'll warn you. You won't end up getting exactly what you're after unless the seller is desperate. If he has decent legal and tax counsel, they'll scream. They will, understandably, try to maximize the sale to the seller's benefit. The seller may be thrilled with your bottom line offer until he realizes what he'll end up taking home from the table. Here is where much of the negotiating give and take comes in.

Know in advance what you're willing to give up without a big fight. Knowing what the seller is in for in the tax department gives you a big edge. If, for example, you know that by re-allocating a particular asset from one spot to another on the financial sheet will save the seller several thousand dollars, you might use this to lower the final purchase price significantly. Just be sure your generosity doesn't cost you more than you're gaining.

On the other hand, you may be willing to bet on your ability to expand the practice enough to make up for any adverse additional tax liability you're going to incur down the line. Giving in somewhere may be the only way you feel you have of placing yourself into what is the most attractive practice you'll ever see. That's a judgment call on your part. Just be conscious of what you're doing.

One frustrating thing you may find in this process is an apparent willingness of the seller to agree to much of what you've outlined, only to have him back down when he talks to his advisors. What you've originally agreed upon may be out the window. Know where you must draw the line and be prepared to stick to it.

A word of caution. This is not in the least like the familiar, customary residential real estate sale in which escrow money is offered by the buyer as a show of good faith. There, a standard contract is presented to both parties with only minor changes to cover special or unusual circumstances. There's a generally understood knowledge of what is transferred from seller to buyer, and how that transfer is to take place.

Because there's no such general agreement on the way a practice sale should be structured, each contract is unique. For this reason, to offer escrow money before all details are worked out is hazardous. It implies an agreement to terms not yet specified, something that can leave you holding a very large, very empty sack. Do not let yourself be talked into prematurely putting out any cash for any reason.

The same holds true for signing an interim agreement. These innocent looking documents may outline some very general, even vague terms which can come back to haunt you later. That interim agreement can be just as binding as a final detailed contract and may contain provisions you can't live with. Getting it torn up may be expensive. This doesn't mean you should flatly refuse any such document couched as a serious letter of intent. It does mean you shouldn't sign blindly.

You should also be wary of a "standard" contract presented to you by a broker. Though it's the eighth verse of the same old song you've seen before in these pages, get your attorney to look it over carefully. Have your accountant do the same. Don't be afraid to make any changes you feel will help your position. If you'd like, have your own attorney rewrite the entire thing, incorporating all the objections you have to the way the agreement is structured.

One item which neither buyer nor seller generally pays great attention to is the "non-performance" section of the contract. You'll find this little gem hidden on a back page when the seller is carrying the note on the practice. You both know the interest rate you'll be paying and maybe what penalties will be assessed for a late payment. No one at the table expects this part of a contract to ever be brought to bear, so everyone glosses over it.

The seller, for his part, devoutly prays this bit of language will merely languish in limbo until the contract terms are fulfilled. He has no urgent desire to step back into harness next year and resume control of the practice. In fact, the thought may give him nightmares.

You, the buyer, have every confidence you can make the practice pay off handsomely. The last thing you're thinking of is the possibility you're wrong. But what if you are? What if you find after a few months you're just squeaking through? What if you run into a temporary cash flow problem?

Most sellers, as mortgage holders, in this situation will be quite understanding. They don't want the practice back. They've either retired or assumed other commitments which would make foreclosure as much of a disaster for them as it would be for you. But what price are you going to pay for their leniency if you do find yourself in a bind?

Read the fine print! Does a missed payment get tacked on to the end of the contract? What is the interest rate going to be on that payment? How are future payments to be allocated in such a situation?

I bring this to your attention since I have sitting in a basket on the top of my desk right now a contract which has no clear picture of these terms. This was a sale where both buyer and seller agreed quickly about almost everything. In fact, they developed a real friendship by the time the practice was transferred.

Due to a series of unavoidable misadventures, the buyer missed several payments immediately after the purchase. He explained the situation to the seller and the two informally agreed he could just tack them onto the end of the payment schedule. The seller did agree not to foreclose, preferring instead to let interest accrue on the past due amount.

The trouble was, the contract was fuzzy on this point and the seller unfortunately passed away before the end of the contract period. Now the heirs and the hapless buyer have almost declared war on each other over this discrepancy in their understanding. The difference amounts to something like $6000, not a paltry sum for either side.

The probabilities are that both will lose by the time their attorneys get through arguing. Legal fees will eat up any settlement, no matter how it's resolved. Better both parties had this question ironed out in detail in writing before the unhappiness arose.

It also never occurred to either that the contract might be amended by consent of both parties. One quick page of document done at the time of their handshake would've been well worth the $100 or so it would've cost one or both of them.

Another neglected item is the "noncompetition" clause. Here are two examples of poorly written documents which led to difficulty.

The first involved location. A broker, used to doing business in the big city, routinely counseled that 10 airline miles was the distance his contracts usually specified. In an urban setting this was more than sufficient to avoid difficulty for the buyer. Unfortunately this was a rural practice in the wide open West. People often travelled 20 miles for nothing more than groceries. Ten miles didn't even extend to the next town!

In his late 40s, the seller had heart trouble and felt he must retire, so he sold out. At that time he didn't feel *any* clause was necessary. He was through. Finished. Done. But thanks to modern medicine, he was feeling great in about six months. His doctor gave him the go-ahead to do whatever he felt like tackling. Including a full day in a dental office.

The seller re-read the contract and promptly opened an office in the next town, a mere 15 miles down the road. The buyer found his patient load suddenly dropped to little more than half what it had been. It didn't help his digestion one bit to know there wasn't a thing he could do about the situation. The seller may not have behaved in the best ethical tradition of the profession, but what he did was legal. I assure you they sit as far from each other as possible at dental meetings.

The second disaster occurred when a well-meaning attorney inadvertently tied the noncompetition clause to the term of the note the buyer gave the seller. As long as the buyer owed money, he was safe.

A year later the buyer came into a fair amount of money, courtesy of an uncle. Looking for a good investment, he decided the best was in himself. He paid off the note, not remembering or maybe not understanding the obscure legal wording of the agreement. It took the seller all of a month to open an office across the street. The buyer had some very lean times.

These two examples point out that you're not always dealing with angels. A small proportion of our profession is populated by opportunists who are only out for themselves, and to perdition with the rest of the world. Others hear only what they want to hear. For that reason, if no other, be sure your agreement is spring-water clear.

One other issue that's scarcely addressed in most agreements is what restrictions you, the buyer, are under if you can't make the practice work for you. Can you resell it to lighten the debt you're facing? Can you sublet the premises? What are your own noncompetition restrictions in the contract? These and other similar matters should be addressed before you pick up the ballpoint.

While I've only outlined briefly three of the potential sins you might commit when signing a contract blindly, there are many more. Let the small horror stories used as examples alert you to some of the things that can happen to you and act accordingly.

# Chapter 15

# The Partnership, Association Leading To Partnership, And/or Eventual Buyout

This collection of arrangements is really only a specialized subset of a practice purchase. These arrangements do have some large advantages over the simple straightforward purchase in that they routinely allow the patients a chance to see the new person in the office over a number of months or years before they are transferred over.

The mechanics of locating a practice arrangement of this sort are about the same as finding a practice for sale outright. Brokers, university listings, dental association assistance, supply house referrals, and classified ads in dental journals all have offerings.

Choosing the right one for you is no easier than it is locating a practice for outright immediate sale. It may actually be harder. The basic difference is you'll be working for (or with) the other doctor for quite some time.

While being cooped up in a few hundred square feet with somebody you detest personally for a few months is something you may be able to withstand for the sake of your own advancement, doing so for an extended period may be a different matter. For this reason it's crucial you get to know your potential boss or co-worker pretty well before you spread ink on the back page of a contract.

In fact, if you don't like the other party or parties, get out of town before you end up making everybody miserable. What's being offered may be a good deal for someone else, but it isn't for you. It's probably warrantable that you'll be unhappy later if you don't.

Having belabored that point, let's turn to some of the other mundane issues that may arise in this type of arrangement. There are several.

The first is the end result. Are you to eventually become the sole owner of the practice, or are you to be the second stringer until the elder statesman finally retires? I pose this question since many dentists in their late 40s or early 50s make noises about retirement in "just a few years." Sometimes this open-ended pronouncement may end up meaning as much as 25 or 30 years.

The trouble is that retirement keeps getting pushed back as decision time approaches. With these individuals, it takes a serious debilitating illness or outright death to push them out from behind the dental chair. For this reason, a time frame is essential for all concerned. Even if the older practitioner does continue on well past normal retirement age, an understanding of exactly when control of the practice is passed to the buyer is necessary.

The same thing applies to advancement from associate status to a partnership. This may be measured in a number of ways. The most common is using time as the test. For example, Dr. A agrees to take in Dr. B as an associate with the understanding that in two years B will be a junior partner. Then in five years the partnership will be an equal one. Further, A will agree to bow out in an additional five years, either by outright retirement or by assuming a subservient position in the office.

These phases may be linked to a transfer of money. For instance, B may have to come up with cash at each step of the way. Failure to exercise this option on B's part means he will stay at the level he's already attained.

This provision should be looked at in some detail before any other issues regarding this type of transfer are discussed. Any provision for goodwill valuation that's contained in such a contract should be based on the practice as it stands before B enters. Failing that, the increase in goodwill should be linked to A's investment and risk in taking on B initially.

Why? It may be that the introduction of B dramatically increases the worth of the practice in a very short time. B should not be forced to pay A for the entire advantage A gains from B being around. An exception might be an allowance for inflation as measured by the government's index or other standard index. Another might be a reasonable return on A's investment over the interim.

This provision may be partially offset by one covering tangible assets as detailed earlier. The tangible asset value may change considerably in the intervening time between B's first coming into the office and his actually buying into it. A reasonable approach might be to use appraised value, trade-in value, depreciated value plus any salvage value in fully depreciated equipment, a combination of these values, or some other mutually agreed figure.

In many situations Dr. A may be justified in inflating one or more of the goodwill figures to more fully compensate him for the risk he took in hiring B. It's quite possible B was a liability initially, not producing enough to cover the expenses he cost A. This is reasonable as long as B's aware of it up front. What this figure should be ought to be spelled out in exquisite detail in the initial hiring contract.

When using a time frame for advancement, the advancement should, within reason, be at B's option so that failure to come up with the required cash on the dot will not place him in the position of being in danger of being tossed out on his ear.

One alternative to the time method of advancement might be the attainment of production or gross collection figures. For example, when B's production or gross receipts meet a certain percentage of A's, the option clause kicks in. This arrangement may or may not be tied in some way to a time frame before which such an option cannot be exercised. This is done to prevent go-getter B, who just inherited a chunk of money, from booting A out of the office prematurely.

Other alternative measuring devices may be the number of active patients, net income, average billing or production per patient, or any other device that reflects to some extent how much the new doctor is contributing to the practice. The possibilities are limited only by the imagination of the parties involved.

A big issue to be considered is an "out" clause. Any arrangement between a buyer and seller of any sort constitutes a binding contract. The seller may, during the initial period of association, actually take something of a financial beating by having a junior associate in the office.

He's not going to be happy if Junior, who is still an associate and has little or no financial interest in the practice, suddenly decides the grass is greener in the office lawn two blocks down the road.

Unless Junior protects himself in the initial employment contract, Senior may sue and collect everything up to and including the retreaded shoes used when Junior walked out on him. Senior may be well justified in demanding a "buyout" provision in the employment contract to keep Junior from essentially robbing his patient files, but there should be limits.

There's no magic formula to cover this situation. Your value or liability to the seller depends on so many factors that each specific arrangement must be custom tailored to fit. I only caution you to be sure both your rights and liabilities are spelled out.

One subset of this "out" business is a noncompetition agreement. This should apply to you initially while the seller is still in control and apply with equal vigor to the seller later on. You don't want your friendly seller to sometime hand over the keys and move across the hall the next day as a competitor.

If you're moving into a strange town and office, it might be a good idea to have an initial honeymoon period where no anti-competition restrictions are placed on you. It's germane to remember that an engagement nearly always precedes a marriage, and very few breach of promise suits are filed in this day and age, probably for a very good reason.

It's much better to have an understanding that no matter how eager both you and the seller are to enter into an arrangement, there may be trouble on the near horizon.

You might even try for something more than just your future freedom, though you may have trouble negotiating it. By this, I mean you also might want some sort of compensation if the seller backs out down the line.

It's just possible you may go to a fair amount of personal expense to get set up in that office, to say nothing of time. It'd be a distinct financial setback if, after a few months, you drove in to work one morning only to find the seller had, without any justification, changed the locks overnight.

In one instance I am aware of, the buyer/associate was not protected in any manner in the contract. The seller backed out of the contract, something he was apparently legally allowed to do under a provision of the contract. He then invoked the noncompetition clause that was present. The lawyers had a field day. The buyer was eventually able to prove his dismissal was not really justified, but the award he ultimately received wasn't sufficient to truly compensate him for the time lost out of his professional career. Had there been a clear penalty clause, it's just possible the seller might have thought twice before acting.

The third tricky point concerns the premature death or disability of the seller before all provisions of the contract are fulfilled. Presumably you'll be dealing with an older practitioner whose potential for adjusting the mortality tables downward is greater than yours.

You and the senior partner may be fast friends or even relatives, but at this juncture you may well be dealing with others who don't have the same esteem for you. Sometimes they're only interested in milking an estate for every buck they can. If you get stepped on in the process, that's your tough luck. Have your rights and opportunities on paper.

On the other hand, the seller may want some assurances that your heirs aren't going to tie up the practice for years if something happens to you. Come to an understanding of just what everyone's options are in such an unhappy circumstance and make sure it gets into your contract.

By now you're probably convinced I'm looking for trouble in every arrangement two humans make. Believe it or not, I do trust my fellow man more than I've indicated. Most of the horror stories contained in this chapter are exceptions to the rules of the game.

Nevertheless, I've learned over the years that two people don't always interpret an agreement the same way. Even the smallest of misunderstandings may rankle one or both parties involved. That's why I feel it's best to add a couple of extra pages to your contract. It may not be necessary, but it's better to head off trouble that doesn't occur than to deal with it later.

I assure you, the last thing you want is a seller or partner who's had his feelings hurt. Equally important, you want to be a happy buyer. Both make life easier for you.

# Chapter 16

# Space Sharing

For the dentist who has little or no financial backing, personal resources, or access to significant loan money, the idea of sharing the space and equipment of another practitioner sounds appealing. You're your own boss with full control over your professional decisions and an unfettered opportunity to build a practice from scratch.

Sometimes you'll even get a small boost from the other occupant of the office. Your "roomie" may have a plate full, but not quite enough to go out and hire an associate. More rarely, you'll run across an older practitioner who wants to cut back on responsibility, and hours.

On the other side of the ledger, this may be a way for a beginning dentist to whittle an oppressive overhead down to manageable proportions and at the same time reap some of the benefits just listed.

Because this approach may appeal to you either as the primary party offering the use of your office or as the one stepping in as a sub-renter, this chapter will take a less adversarial tone than that used in the rest of this book. A few of the hazards of sharing space will be presented from a neutral corner.

There are a number of reasons for taking on someone by using a space-sharing plan as a vehicle. Cutting expenses is the most obvious. As just mentioned, an older doctor may want to ease his work load but not want the responsibility or restrictive structure of having an associate and being saddled with the increased overhead and paperwork.

Alternatively, he or she may feel it's a way to informally try out someone who might later want to take over the practice or become a partner. They might even feel it's a way to justify buying a batch of fancy expensive equipment that isn't currently economically sound to install. Whatever the reason, though, the hazards and rewards of space sharing are fairly uniform.

On the surface the idea of sharing space and equipment appears ideal. For the dentist coming in, there's little or no front money required, lower overhead than there would be in a solo office, ready access on site for coverage in case an occasion arises requiring taking a day or two off, an office open as many as 15 hours a day to make appointments and provide patient support, the possibility of an incipient patient base built in—and on and on.

It sounds like a dream come true on both sides. Often it is. Other times that dream is similar to the fitful mental images initiated by that suspect fried pickle and green chili supper sponsored by the local Fraternal Order of the Wounded Bear club to raise money for their annual beer bust picnic. In more straightforward terms, the arrangement can be a disaster.

There are several potential sources of conflict that will lead to divorce in such an arrangement. The first and greatest of these is the lack of a written agreement spelling out the limitations and responsibilities of each party.

To illustrate, let's assume Dr. A and Dr. B meet and decide they can benefit from sharing quarters. Neither is particularly fond of the idea of a true merger or partnership—at least not for the present. They have lunch, maybe a drink after work, talk it over for a few minutes, and shake hands.

What they've discussed is no more than the general office hours each will keep, what help each will supply, and a vague understanding they'll split expenses.

Since it's A's office, A chooses the prime hours for the full week. B isn't really thrilled about this, but says nothing. He'd like an evening or two off with his family instead of dragging home after the toddler's in bed. He goes along though. Beggars can't be choosers and B feels he's got a good deal overall. Still, the silver cloud has a bit of tarnish already, and it's only been a week.

There are other dissatisfactions. A's assistants don't really love coming to work an hour earlier than before. Getting off earlier is great, but they're all having to forgo that great long lunch hour in order to compress A's day down to a manageable size. Eating a bologna sandwich in between loading the sterilizer and cleaning the bloody spots off the floor in the main operatory isn't anyone's idea of gracious dining.

B's crew isn't thrilled, either. They come to work in the middle of the afternoon and don't get dinner until much later than they're accustomed to. It interferes with their social life something fierce. There's a bit of a pay differential because of the odd hours, but not enough to make them eager to forgo the more pleasurable things of life.

They're not overjoyed that the office is never really clean when they arrive for the evening shift. The morning bunch has to get out in a hurry to make way for them, so nothing is shipshape. When things have been hectic early on, they occasionally find they're short of instruments. The late crowd retaliates by leaving their own mess for the morning drudges. It isn't long before Dr. A is having heartburn. (B already is taking antacid.)

A has other troubles in the cleaning department, too. The outside janitorial service that hits twice a week to do a really good job on the floors has to adjust its schedule to fit into the new routine. The charge goes up significantly to cover the inconvenience. A keeps muttering it's all right since the expenses are split now and it's still costing less than it did before—but it still rankles.

Major disagreements arise over what an "expense" actually is and which ones should be shared equally. B spends a lot of time on the phone to an out-of-town laboratory. A doesn't appreciate being tagged with half the cost of chatter like this.

B in turn bridles when A's accountant suggests that B should be charged half the current depreciation write-off on the equipment and leasehold improvements. The idea sounds good to A, though. After all, B is causing considerable wear and tear on the chairs. That should be worth something.

Worse, A isn't happy about the front desk situation. Practice growth slowed perceptibly when B came on the scene. A has a niggling suspicion B's receptionist is doing what she can to steer new patients to B rather than playing fair during her shift.

The final blowup occurs when A discovers one morning there's no material in the office to take that all-important bite for the fancy five unit bridge. It'd been hard to do a decent preparation on Mrs. Finnikie. B had obviously been raiding the wrong half of the supply cabinet.

A fumes until B shows up all smiles. A demands all B's keys and summarily tosses everyone out on the sidewalk. At the end of the month B receives a bill for a pro-rata share of the expenses for that month.

B's wounded pride and loss of several big bills in patient treatment during the time it took to get into another office lead directly to a lawyer who files suit for damages and failure to perform under the pair's oral contract. Two former amenable colleagues are now sworn enemies who go out of their way to damage each other's reputation.

You may be asking yourself if there are really two highly trained, well educated people in this country who can be that petty, that stupid. The truth is, it's possible. I've seen most of the elements in this horror story played out in a trio of offices.

Prevention of disaster is simple. There are two elements. The first is, *get it all in writing.* The other is equally straightforward. *Understand what you're signing.*

Do you need a 20-page legal document with "whereas" and "therefore" scattered, notary seals affixed, and the whole mess recorded at the county clerk's office? Probably not. It depends on the ultimate fairness and good faith of both parties and their willingness to see the other's point of view. But there is still a crying need for a written agreement.

This agreement should spell out precisely what the duties and responsibilities of each party are. It should include, but not necessarily be limited to:

1. What a shared office expense actually is, who is ultimately responsible for it and what office expenses shouldn't be in the common pool.

2. What supplies are to be shared and which are the exclusive property of each.

3. How new patients are to be shared. Should each doctor have his own phone line, or is the existing service to be shared? Comment—there's a bit less possibility for disagreement with separate lines.

4. How do you avoid trouble over patient scheduling? For instance, should, in the above example, both receptionists be paid equally by both doctors, possibly even trading off time slots regularly to help ensure fairness?

5. Who is responsible for physically writing the checks for the office bills, and what are the other party's rights if they aren't taken care of? For instance, if our Dr. A failed to pay the rent and the pair is evicted, does B have any recourse? Does B have the right to see that pertinent bills are current? If I were B, I'd like copies for my files for tax purposes, if for no other reason.

6. How long does B have to pay his or her share of the expenses after being notified of the obligation? Can he or she see any bills in question to verify the figures? Again, a written agreement would forestall any problems here.

7. How much control can Dr. B exert over what is actually spent? If A sees expenses are way down and feels the urgent necessity of a full page ad in the yellow pages touting the office, does B have a say, an outright veto, or the option of not paying the projected share? To be fair, B should probably have the option to not pay a share of this type of bill unless consulted. The same applies to equipment purchases and other similar items.

8. What mechanism is to be used to terminate the agreement? This should be very specific and cover as many eventualities as possible.

For example, what happens to B if A piles his car into a bridge abutment on the way home? An unpleasant thought, but such things do happen occasionally. What happens if B runs off to Tahiti with his assistant and leaves A with a batch of unpaid bills? More commonly, what happens when one decides it's just not working out?

Vehicles such as life insurance, bonding, periodically updated buyout or buy/sell agreements, reserve accounts, contingency lease transfers, and others are available to cover eventualities like this. They don't occur often, but there's no use taking anything for granted.

9. If a dispute arises that's not covered by the agreement, what procedure is there to settle it without someone immediately instituting court proceedings?

One special circumstance should be dealt with here. That's where two dentists band together and both purchase equipment to open and outfit a space shared office. They may even jointly pay remodeling costs on the leased space.

What they're really doing is forming a loose partnership to jointly be responsible for the facility, but are maintaining discrete professional lives. In this situation, it's imperative to reduce everything to writing, including disposition of the assets in the case of disability or death of one of the partners.

Precise details should be spelled out as to who retains the premises in the event one of them wants out of the arrangement later on. By now, you should've read enough about pitfalls and hazards to work up your own disaster story for this situation. I won't bore you with mine.

This last case is one in which you definitely need the legal terminology and the services of a competent, experienced attorney.

I suppose the biggest question is what's fair in a space sharing relationship? What should each party expect? What should each party expect to give up in the way of total freedom to make non-professional office decisions?

Frankly, I wish there was a generic set of answers to this collection of conundrums. The wide diversity of potential arrangements makes a generic answer impossible. There are a few things that will assist in making such an arrangement work more harmoniously.

1. The people involved must like and respect each other personally and professionally.

2. The closer the match in practice philosophy and approach to patients, the better.

3. The better the two staffs get along, the better.

4. The less disposable or consumable supplies are shared—or borrowed—the better.

5. The better the respective spouses get along, the better. This doesn't mean the families must socialize or be bosom buddies. The barest hint of resentment on the part of a spouse can touch off fireworks eventually.

6. If the two have a third party they both respect who is willing to arbitrate disputes, it's a plus.

7. The ability to put past differences aside is a must. A shared dental office is no place to harbor a grudge.

8. A common office manual helps. Some offices go so far as hiring help

jointly even though the assistant is working for and is paid by only one of the doctors.

If all of this discussion of potential difficulties makes the idea sound dismal, don't be disheartened. It can work. Remember, even though half the marriages in this country end in divorce, the other half don't. Many of those that survive are a pure joy to both parties. Simply try to remember not to go into any practice arrangement without knowing what you're in for and what your responsibilities will be.

I might add that many of the initial space—sharing arrangements do end in a true professional marriage—that is, some sort of partnership or group practice. If you think there's even a remote possibility of this in the future, have something in writing to spell out the general terms under which it can take place.

Perhaps the greatest single problem in space sharing is a lack of communication as to what each wants out of the practice he or she is each running, and how the other can help or hinder this goal.

To aid communication, I'd suggest the two doctors actually work a few hours a week together even though it may not be as efficient. They should also arrange joint staff meetings fairly regularly so the two sets of toilers can understand each other's problems.

One successful threesome of space sharers go so far as to swap staff every couple of months for a week. This unusual trio—two men and a woman—have dissimilar practice philosophies, patient approaches, and goals, but they've made it work extremely well by communicating constantly and respecting each other's desires.

To put this relationship in shorthand, ask each of them privately what makes the arrangement click and each will tell you the same thing, "It's not really my doing. The other two bend over backwards to make it work."

Remember, what your expectations may be won't always jibe with those of your office roommate. The best time to solve problems is when they're a possibility, not a crisis. Approach this arrangement with all the caution and consideration you'd give to something you're investing large sums of money in. It's the first step in your future. You should plan with that firmly affixed in your mind.

# Chapter 17

# Involvement With Managed Care

To join or not to join?

Sorry, Shakespeare, for playing games with your famous phrase; but it can't be helped. It all too neatly sums up the dilemma nearly all dentists face today. It's not only whether or not they should sign up with an alternative delivery outfit, but which one. And to what extent.

As you can imagine, your unique location, overhead, staff, patient base, potential, and style of delivery of service will determine whether you can participate in any particular plan and still make a living. To make matters worse, there's the little wild card known as annual review—something that'll materially affect your continued participation and income if you join a plan. Don't count on that plan forever.

Here's an example of what you may be up against. I carefully analyzed one capitation plan offered me some years ago. It would've been a modest money maker, but only if I accepted less than 30 families. Strangely, more participants meant less money in my pocket—until the number of families reached about 200. Then it began to offer the possibility of profits again. With a fairly full schedule already, 200 additional families was too large a load for me to take on.

That was my conclusion for my office. A colleague just a few doors away fattened his retirement account considerably with 100 of those accounts. His basic overhead was similar to mine and so were his general fees. The only difference was his approach to delivering treatment and his handling of the alternative patients. He made it work. I couldn't.

You, as a beginner, also have to consider precisely these same questions.

What makes it worse for you is, you have to make difficult decisions without having a practice baseline to work with.

Don't feel bad about any confusion you may have regarding the subject. In a perusal of recent literature regarding the advantages and disadvantages of managed care to prepare for this section of the book, only one thing was readily discernible. The experts are as confused as everyone else. They can't even fully agree on basic terminology.

Opinions range from a firm belief that it's impossible to make a living by being involved in any form of managed care. There's an equal conviction that no dentist can survive without loading his or her appointment schedule to the rim with these "alternative" patients.

Both sides are right, given the parameters they lay down. The truth is, what's right for one office is totally wrong for the next. To help you make up your mind when faced with this choice as you approach your new practice, a quick review of what's involved is in order.

Before we delve into this subject, though, I feel it only honest to editorialize a moment. I have a bias on this subject which may unintentionally color my advice regarding this issue. I shall do my best to remain scrupulously neutral, but I urge you to be wary in case my opinion slants the discussion.

What is this bias? There's no secret agenda involved, I assure you. It's simply my deep feeling and unswerving conviction that no professional can cut all fees all the time without eventually cutting some aspect of service to patients. Unless, of course, those fees were outlandish to begin with. Sufficient trimming will inevitably lead to a loss of quality in the service being delivered.

It's also my belief that the individual dentists who approach negotiation with any managed care system, no matter what the designation, are at a tremendous disadvantage. My reasoning is as follows: No individual dentist with a six-figure gross has any bargaining leverage at all when dealing with an insurance company, self-insuring corporation, or other health care giant whose cash flow can be measured in billions. These giants don't need you.

If you don't take unquestioningly what they have to offer, they'll find another sucker in the neighborhood to do their bidding on their terms. While it's been reported that contract negotiation is possible, realistically, the probability is remote.

There's another aspect, too. In purely business terms, the monetary risk they take with you or any other contract professional is minimal. You're a single molecule of salt in their ocean.

You, on the other hand, are required to assume the major part of any financial liability which may arise. It's your neck on the block if you elect to treat the patients they underwrite. In fact, some contracts go so far as to require you to defend the insurer in case of foul up. This is true whether the treatment they allow in their schedule of benefits is optimal for a particular patient or not.

Furthermore, they have absolutely no obligation to see you remain financially solvent. They've discovered there's always another hungry supplicant waiting to take over if you throw in the towel.

I freely admit I'm a cynic. To my shame I'm sometimes proud of the label. That doesn't take away the truth of my observation that the milk of human kindness is seldom served in crystal carafes in the plush corporate boardrooms of insurance conglomerates.

We dentists, on the other hand, have never been weaned from the stuff. Many of us are downright addicted to it, making us easy plucking for ambitious executive types interested only in increasingly favorable quarterly reports.

Since this is my attitude, you may wish to consult additional sources when developing your approach to joining a managed care plan. In fact, I'd consider it essential. I shall only urge you to be extremely cautious about taking any information handed you by a three-letter outfit at face value. Only one party in the proposed deal is well guaranteed to make money.

With that editorial out of the way, let's take what I hope is a reasonably dispassionate look at what "managed care" actually means—and how it may fit into your new practice.

Incidentally, even the term "managed care" isn't clearly defined. In the literature designated primarily for consumption by insurers and purchasers of insurance, it refers to any form of insurance, including straightforward reimbursement for fee-for-service.

Other MBA types use the term to cover only those schemes which have a capitation component. The most common understanding of the term among the professions is that it refers to any insurance plan that seeks, by contract with the provider, to cap or otherwise limit the fees collected for services rendered. That's more or less the definition used in this tome.

To simplify what tends to be a bewildering array of options, it's easier to sort them out if you know there are only a pair of basic alternative financing methods. Each has two subdivisions,

The first category is an off-shoot of good old fee-for-service. Subset Number One is nearly traditional in that the only control placed on the insurer's expense is the implementation of a maximum allowance for each service rendered.

Subset Number Two is the PPO. This involves convincing a group of dentists to lower fees in return for having the insurer funnel all the group's patients to them. The reduction may be in the form of a fixed-fee schedule or a discount on the individual dentist's regular fees.

The other main payment method is the capitation scheme. This is generally called an HMO.

Subset Number One here is the open arrangement where the individual dentist contracts with the parent company to provide service to the group for a monthly fee for each subscriber choosing his office.

Subset Number Two here is the closed arrangement where all professional personnel are salaried employees of the HMO. This category is presented for information only. It won't affect you in a true private practice.

Many of these capitation plans may also contain a provision for a copayment, seating fee, or other extra payment for the dentist. When this happens, the plan becomes a hybrid of two or more of the basic payment methods. They may also contain provisions which allow the dentist to offer additional services or more expensive treatment options to the insured patient on a uninsured or partially insured fee-for-service basis. They may even be structured to encourage such an action. We'll examine that little gem shortly.

What's the ideal plan? This depends on who you talk to. For the dentist, the ideal plan would be a capitation program where large numbers of patients sign up with his or her office but never came in. If carried to its ultimate, the dentist wouldn't ever have to go to the office—or even have an office.

For the insurance company, the ideal situation would be a fee-for-service contract with a fixed premium. The insurance company would collect a large payment each month from an employer and, like the above dentist, never have anyone file a claim.

The employer would much prefer to completely avoid carrying health insurance in any form. He'd like a totally healthy work force that didn't have so much as an aspirin in their collective medicine chests. If possible, he'd opt for only sterile employees, thus eliminating that sole remaining spectre of maternity benefits. Dental insurance is the least of his priorities.

Each side is striving to achieve its personal ultimate Nirvana. The dentist, if he or she must work, wants as much for his or her labors as possible. The insurance company wants exactly the opposite. The employer doesn't want to shell out in the first place. The result is a constant jockeying for a better position in the game resulting in a continuing change in plans offered and accepted. Novel combinations of capitation, deductibles, fee ceilings, and co-payments float out of sleek offices in an endless stream.

Instant experts crop up, hawking their infallible answers to current problems, only to find they're obsolete before that lucrative lecture tour is booked. It's no wonder the average dentist is confused. How does he or she make sense out of all this chaos? Let's look.

Most, if not all, "alternative" plans have been, and still are, pitched to the individual dentist on the premise they'll bring in extra fee-for-service patients by widening the patient pool. The corporate peddler may intimate the dentist might not make a great amount of loot from these customers, but the plan is structured so the dentist is assured of not losing, either. This monetary shortfall is theoretically made tolerable by those increased referrals from the plan's enrollees.

Let's investigate this no-loss claim, starting with the PPO concept. There are two assumptions made by the insurer. The first is, the overhead in a dental office runs about 60 percent. Compensation is based on the dentist's return being around 70 percent of personal UCR, which is shorthand for normal fees. Some of the more generous plans may claim a return as much as 80 percent of "normal" fees. If your overhead is higher then their norm, you make less. If a fee in your fee schedule exceeds their statistical limits, they impose a ceiling on that fee, further cutting the potential profit.

To keep expenses down, the insurer generally insists the patient pay part of this reduced fee as a co-payment. The copayment usually varies with the procedure. Another limit is the (LEAT) least expensive alternative treatment. For example, the insurance company will authorize a partial denture but not a fixed bridge. This has a net effect of dragging down the dentist's profit potential further than expected.

Capitation (HMO) plans work differently. When first proposed by government planners back in the 70s, they were called radical new ideas. The truth is they had their roots in China thousands of years ago.

In that culture, healers were paid only when the patient was well. If the patient got sick, the money stopped until the patient was up and around again. Today's concept isn't all that different, even though the current basic medical emphasis tends to be on treatment rather than prevention. Here's how they work for us.

The contracting dentist is paid a fixed fee, usually monthly, for each patient enrolled in his practice. Patients may be subdivided into several groups according to age, sex, education level, and job title. One outfit goes so far as to consider the patient's zip code. Compensation for each subgroup will vary according to some demographic study the insurance company developed. Families are often discounted. The validity of such a ranking system is open to serious questioning. Don't wager your acreage on it working in your behalf.

Many of these plans also provide a safety valve in case of overutilization. This usually takes the form of an hourly fee for any excessive time spent by the dentist in treating the plan's patients. The insurer determines this based on a schedule that lists how long it supposedly takes to do each procedure. The extra payment kicks in when certain criteria based on time per registered patient is exceeded. The time span usually considered is quarterly.

The calculations are convoluted and vary from plan to plan. Theoretically, if you see enough patients and beat the clock often enough, you'll be well rewarded. Conversely, dawdle over many of these patients and you'll starve.

Capitation plans offer other rich areas for creative planning on the part of insurers. Hybrid cross-breeding between PPO and HMO concepts may produce a plan with a capitation base, a seating fee charged to the patient, deductibles, ceiling caps, a varying copayment on some procedures, and who knows what else. Trying to analyze some of these for profit potential is something that'll give you a major migraine.

With both concepts and the hybrids, any treatment not authorized by the insurer generally becomes the patient's full responsibility. Though not widely advertised by the insurer, this creates an opportunity for additional profit for the dentist.

The classic example would be convincing a patient of the advantages of cosmetic dentistry. Naturally, this would be paid for by the patient at the customary commercial rate. The same principle applies if the patient's treatment is restricted by an exclusion for pre-existing conditions.

Other, possibly questionable, opportunities for additional income may occur even when a current condition is covered. Here a bit of lesser known alphabetizing is invoked by the dentist. This one is LEAPAET. This tongue twister is short for "least expensive professionally adequate ethical treatment." It's truly a slippery ethical decision made by the dentist. Here's how it works: A patient breaks a filling—a fairly large amalgam, for instance. The insurance company will allow a replacement amalgam or composite, invoking LEAT. The dentist then trots out LEAPAET and tells the patient he'll put in the filling, but in his professional judgment the tooth really needs a crown. If the patient goes along with the recommendation, it's the patient's responsibility to pay for it, or at least the additional cost. This effectively creates, at least temporarily, a fee-for-service patient from the "plan" patient.

What the pure ethical position really is here, I'm not sure. To my knowledge no one has yet divined the perfect answer to the knotty problem of just when a filling ceases to be "adequate" or a crown "necessary."

The bottom line is, few insurers object to this arrangement. Sometimes they're off the hook for the amalgam, which saves them money. Unless a dentist consistently and grossly overtreats a large segment of the plan's patients, they'll probably secretly applaud the enterprising dentist. They truly don't mind a dentist making a profit—especially if it also increases their own profit margin.

The insurer's representative may or may not tell you of these little tricks when he's doing his selling job. Make it a point to ask how the company views these arrangements and how cooperative they'll be when such a situation arises.

Another argument you may hear to convince you to sign up is the one concerning "unused chair time." It goes something like this: Suppose your office has three chairs. Your overhead is $60 an hour. It follows that every hour each chair is unoccupied you're out an unneccessary $20.00, plus any profit that might be gleaned from having that chair full. It would be worse if you only had two chairs. You'd be costing yourself $30.00. By filling your empty chair with the plan's patients, you're really not adding to your overhead, and anything you take in is nearly all profit.

There's only one flaw in this argument. The validity of the premise applies only if you're able to actually treat two or three patients at the same time. The concept may work for physicians who turn over a goodly portion of their workload to ancillaries. We can't. At least we can't if we stay within the laws governing our practices. Watch out you don't fall for this pitch.

So far, we've looked at three sides of what is a four-way tug of war—the combatants being the patient, the employer, the insurer, and the dentist. Hopefully, you now have some understanding of how each strives to gain the upper hand and how they'll use you for their own ends if you let them. We've also seen an instance or two in which the game may be turned to the dentist's advantage.

What we haven't looked at is the occasionally participating onlooker. He's an intermittent fifth player in this game that's something of a wild card. He also sometimes acts as referee. Who is he? Government.

Government is the umpire, rule maker, and player in this contest. To carry the sports analogy a bit further, the government is very much like the playground spoiled brat who owns the ball the game's being played with. When the game doesn't go to his liking, he changes the rules! If you object, he'll take his ball and go home. It's much the same here.

Government advanced, promoted, and heavily subsidized the early experiments in HMO concepts. Through the vehicle of Medicare and associated programs, it has set standards throughout the medical community. Many regulations and restrictions, both federal and state, were promulgated to gain partial control over other aspects of the healing arts. These rules also apply to our profession. New rules are imposed almost daily.

For this reason, you should keep a close eye on what comes out of Washington and your nearby state capitol. The decision you make today about managed care participation may not be valid the first of next week. It pays handsomely to be an astute political observer, if not an outright activist.

Now that you have some idea of the rules the game is played with, it's time to see whether or not you want to go on the field. What you need to do is assess your chances for landing on the winning team. This means it's back to checking out the specific details that apply to you.

As already mentioned, most, if not all, plans are pitched to the individual dentist on the premise they'll bring in extra fee-for-service patients by widening the patient pool. By signing on, you're supposed to create additional referrals. Whether it's a valid marketing tool for the dentist involved is a question mark we'll look at as we go along.

As we've discussed, there are infinite variations and combinations of each of the two basic approaches to managed care. The point is, few of the final figures are as remunerative as the traditional fee-for-service arrangement. The question then becomes, which, if any, alternate proposals are acceptably profitable for you?

In order to arrive at some sort of answer, you need to know what it's going to cost you to deliver your wares. That's your starting point. To come up with this figure, I refer you to the chapter on fees. It contains detailed instructions for arriving at your actual cost, both per hour and per procedure.

Let me digress for a second. A great deal of the insurance company figures for compensation are based on full utilization of a dental office for 1,650 hours a year. As I pointed out previously, it's extremely doubtful that many dentists are actually putting in that much chair time annually.

Since hourly fixed overhead varies inversely with the number of hours worked, increasing the time you labor each week can make joining a program a more realistic financial venture. You may also reduce your effective hourly overhead by splitting expenses in a space-sharing or group arrangement. Whether you wish to employ either of these strategies is strictly up to you. They're merely options you might consider.

Once you have your overhead figure, you can begin to make comparisons. Or can you? You, my eager beginner, are in for some real fun. Here's why.

Let's start with PPO concepts first, although some of the statements will apply to capitation situations as well.

It makes sense that the more procedures you do an hour, the less the overhead charge is for each procedure. If you're buying into a practice which already has as part of its base one or more alternate contracts, it's comparatively simple to conduct an audit—provided there are adequate records.

If there aren't, you may have to do some reconstruction from patient charts and the appointment book to learn how long it takes to do each procedure in that office. The usual missing section of the puzzle is the time factor.

There's a hidden catch. What's the time it will take *you* to do the procedure? Do not assume you will be able to function at the same rate established by your predecessor. He or she has probably had years to perfect a technique of efficient treatment delivery. The assistants are trained to work within those parameters—his, not yours. The office is set up for their collective convenience—not yours.

Here's an example that applies to both an existing office and a new one. Unless you've already sharpened all your skills, you may flounder when trying to do a 30-minute crown prep, including impressions and temporaries. For what it's worth, it can be done in far less time, though I'd hate to have the result graded by a critical university professor.

In case you've missed what I'm driving at, here it is. In any situation where you're operating with a set fee schedule, you must be able to make your expenses, plus something extra for your wallet. If, in the case of the crown, the allowance is $200 and your hourly overhead is $200, you must perform the entire procedure in less than an hour. Enough less that there's time to start the next patient. That's how it'll have to be if you plan to make money.

The time factor thus becomes critical in your analysis. If you're opening your own office, you've hopefully already learned how efficient you can be. If you cannot do the work in less than what the insurer seems to think is proper, you must pass by the dubious opportunity of joining his club.

Analyze a good sampling of the most common procedures. If your analysis shows you'll make money on most of them, you're probably on fairly safe ground. As demonstrated earlier, nearly all offices lose money on something.

Just don't cut it too fine.

Capitation plans present a somewhat different challenge. To repeat, in its simplest form, a company agrees to pay you a fixed amount for each patient enrolled in their plan that chooses your office. Immediately two unknown factors are introduced.

The first is the actual number of people who'll pick your name out of the bowler. Initially the company may arbitrarily assign an agreed-upon group to you on the basis of geography or other criteria. The classic rub is, these patients are nearly always free to make another choice at any time.

The result? In three months you may have twice as many as you bargained for—or nearly none at all. Your hard work in making projections about the feasibility of joining the plan sail out into the bleachers somewhere.

The second unknown is the utilization rate. All of the patients on your list may come in for major treatment—or they may stay away in flocks while the company continues to send you a fat check each and every month.

As previously intimated, some companies will make allowances for increased utilization. Others will rate each potential patient according to predicted utilization, then make a different payment for each category.

The theory behind this latter situation is that the more educated a patient is and the more responsible a job a patient has, the more that patient will take care of his or her teeth. Conversely, the janitor partaking of the plan isn't supposed to give a canned fig about his oral cavity. You are compensated accordingly. In real life, this won't always pan out.

Another drawback is, you may be required to provide services you would otherwise farm out to a specialist. If you do so without sufficient justification, you may be required to pick up the specialist's fee. I remember turning down one otherwise comparatively generous plan a number of years ago that would have required me to provide orthodontic treatment—something I was totally unsuited for.

My potential malpractice liability could've run into the extremely large-bill category in a hurry if I'd tried bending wire without knowing what I was doing. It would've been just as foolish to offer to pay for several dozen youngster's winning smiles.

Regarding those specialists. You may have to refer to those offered or authorized by the plan. The reputation of one or more specialists on the insurer's "approved" list may be sorry or they may be downright incompetent. Yes, there are a few around.

If you refer a patient to one of them and the treatment goes sour, you might be on the hook in a courtroom for not using due care in choosing your referral. You might have a hard time shifting the blame onto the insurer because of the terms of the contract you signed.

That leads nicely into the spot to advise you to understand every word and punctuation mark of that contract before you sign. Learn exactly what your responsibilities are. Learn how you opt out. Learn what your liabilities are with the "hold harmless" lingo.

Study that mass of paper. Have your attorney go over it. Fax a copy to the ADA people to analyze it for you. What you might save will probably pay for a couple of year's worth of dues. Once you receive their input, take it back to your own attorney to have the ADA comments translated into what applies in your state. Then, and only then, do you sign.

Unfortunately, all of this doesn't answer the lead question about whether *you* should join. Perhaps the following observations will assist you in gaining additional perspective.

One large drawback to most plans is you have to take all comers. The limited freedom you normally have to reject a patient for whatever cause is nearly completely lost. Some of these patients can be real pills, demanding fee-for-service treatment and consideration for cut rate prices. This may be due to the insurer not explaining the plan properly. That matters not. You're the one in the path of their ire.

Because you must handle these managed care patients differently than you will your fee-for-service folks, it follows that they won't routinely be as happy with you as others might. This means they're less likely to use glowing terms when talking to their friends. Translation, the referrals you might expect aren't going to be as great as you might've expected. What they're more likely to do is, if they find you less repugnant than the other dentists providing service under the plan, refer other plan members to you. This may or may not be something that makes your day a sunny one.

With some plans there may be penalties imposed for not being on the spot seven days a week. The mere fact you're in bed with a raging fever is no excuse. Spending the weekend in continuing education class to maintain your license is no excuse. In many plans there are no contract provisions for farming out emergencies or having another dentist cover for you when you're sick or on vacation. Even if you're in a space-sharing or other arrangement or have an associate, unless your cohort also subscribes to the same plan, he or she can't take over temporarily. If he or she did, you could be out on your tailbone and pay dearly for getting the bounce.

One contract I saw a few years ago was so restrictive that even another contract dentist couldn't cover for you. Worse, no matter what the patient called the office about, the patient was to be seen within 24 hours. Or else. If a patient wanted his teeth cleaned on Christmas morning, you'd better by golly do it or suffer the penalties.

When considering adding managed care patients to your practice, you should ask yourself how they'll fit into your concept of private practice and the goals you've set for yourself. Will you be operating two distinct practice types, or will two radically different treatment modalities blend for you? Will you schedule the two groups separately, or mix them?

While any going practice can absorb a dozen or so stray managed care discount bodies without dislocating anything, having a large percentage of your patients in managed care could conceivably wreck your carefully conceived long-term plans. There's no question you'll have to approach the two groups quite differently. Can you do it successfully in just one office? Do you have the personality to do it? Will your assistants be able to cope?

You also need to ask yourself how stable the alternative contract is. I recall seeing the figures on a practice that was completely geared for, and heavily into, serving one managed care company. When the plan was cancelled by the employer, the doctor's net income immediately dropped from just under $90,000 to less than $18,000. I need not detail the dislocation that caused.

Therefore, you need to carefully note what your options are if the company cancels your contract. For example, how much notice will you receive? Is there any severance pay? How is work in progress to be handled? Equally important, you need to fully understand your responsibilities if you do the walking.

You should understand what provisions there are in the insurer's master contract with the employer for renewal, how long the present contract will run, what alterations in the terms are allowable in the interim, and how the contract may be renewed. Ask how these things affect you. They will, you know.

Don't overlook the little details like the time lag before you're paid. For instance, if one capitation plan pays in advance and the other pays on the fifteenth of the following month, you're looking at a 45-day differential. In the latter situation you might have to borrow money to meet your bills until the first check comes. You'll be playing catch-up for quite some time if utilization is fairly heavy.

The same situation should be investigated in a PPO contract. It could be as much as three months before you see your money. Your accountant will tell you this isn't ideal. In simple language, they're using your money—a situation not too far removed from your handing them an additional discount.

Though mentioned earlier, I cannot emphasize strongly enough to be cautious about any "hold harmless" provisions of that contract. Your own malpractice insurance won't cover the insurer in case of trouble, but that contract might require you to.

Further, look carefully for a provision that takes you out of the picture if someone sues the insurance company or the employer directly. There's no gain in you offering to pay for their lawsuit, something several current contracts stipulate.

With capitation plans, you need to be careful to join a group with a track record good enough to ensure the companies they sign up will stick with them. The reason is, you're in for the long haul if you plan on eventually making money. Most current dental capitation plans are designed to provide decent payment to you only for maintenance service. Period.

This means you'll have to put the group's people in good shape and educate them to appreciate preventive home care. This'll probably be done at minimal profit, or possibly a loss. Only by retaining those patients for a long time can you hope to come out ahead long term. Hence the need for both group and contract stability.

The possible exception to this is when the group's enrollees are fairly young and already in good shape. Remember the discussion in the chapter on locations? They're also more likely to have the proper mind-set for doing the maintenance thing. If you run across this situation, you're more likely to come out ahead in a relative hurry.

Should you join one of these plans out of fear they'll siphon off all the patients in town and leave you in the cold? Not necessarily. There are a number of things currently working in your favor.

In the climate that exists at the time this is being written, it appears the saturation level for dental insurance has about hit its peak. Companies currently providing dental insurance to employees are on a cost-cutting binge. Few outfits that don't already offer dental insurance are likely to voluntarily increase their overhead.

Additionally, labor unions, the prime movers in obtaining ever-increasing fringe benefits, are on the wane. A few years ago they controlled about a third of the total work force. Currently that number is hovering near 10 percent.

Their current thrust is to see their remaining members have some sort of a job, and to perdition with the lace edges on the contract. Seeing their members smile with perfect teeth is not a priority. They want their members to eat. If they have to gum their food, it's better than shipping them off to the bread line.

Depending on who's figures you trust, between 40 percent and 50 percent of the people in this country now have some form of dental insurance. Most of that is straight fee-for-service indemnity. Less than 20 percent of those covered are in some form of managed care. This means at least 80 percent of the potential patients out there can be classified as traditional. That makes the picture look far less bleak than it's often painted.

Further, much of this alternate care is congregated in restricted areas of the country. In small towns, even traditional fee-for-service contracts are rare. Restrictive legislation in several states has made the alternate concept unattractive to employers and insurers alike.

If you're statistically minded, you might take heart in the following observation. The latest figures available state that overall health care costs the U.S. population about $800 billion annually. The dental component of that is somewhat over $40 billion, or around 5 percent. That $800 billion represents about 15 percent of the total funds Americans have available to spend.

When you figure just what percentage of that total paycheck, including benefits, actually goes into our collective dental coffers, it's only a fraction of a single percent. To put this in perspective, our bit of that Gross National Product probably still compares more to the amount spent on pets than any other treasured slice of the American dream.

My strictly personal opinion is that a fairly sizeable number of people will be willing to forgo their "free" managed care rat maze and spend the odd buck in a dental office where they feel they're treated as if they really mattered—especially when they see it's not costing them too big a chunk of their disposable income.

The point? You don't *have* to hit the panic switch the minute an insurance representative knocks on your door. You generally have the luxury of saying no if you wish. There's enough of a traditional pie out there for you to bite into. In most areas of the country, you don't have to worry about starving to death if you don't rush out and sign up. Your share of the aforementioned pie is still undigested.

What about government intervention? My answer needs a disclaimer as follows: The opinions expressed in the following paragraph or two are strictly my own analysis.

Government, especially federal, has long refused to include dentistry as an essential part of any health care scheme it's enacted. As long as there's pressure to reduce fiscal spending, it's unlikely there'll be major expansion of subsidized dental programs. Indeed, there may be reductions in those limited ones already in place.

Further, in the present business climate, legislatures of all ilk aren't about to incur the ire of large masses of employers by mandating they provide additional insurance to their employees. Such a move would be tantamount to political suicide. It would be a most courageous act. Courageous acts are something politicians are terrified of committing.

For these reasons and others, I think you're safe in assuming the basic dental status quo will prevail for the foreseeable future. Managed care contracts may continue to make modest inroads into traditional insurance with ever decreasing cost advantages for the employer. However, they will not completely replace current traditional insurance, nor supplant good old patient-paid fee-for-service.

The same is true of medical HMO operations. Up until now, much of the fiscal advantage they've enjoyed has been due to cost shifting on the part of the individual doctors who contract with them. There's a limit to how long this cost shifting can continue.

There's one other thing the social planners forgot. That's patient satisfaction. As the squeeze continues, patients may not hold still for being treated like penned cattle. They may not remain passive when an insurance clerk overrides their doctor's judgment. As more horror stories appear on the tube, dissatisfaction will escalate considerably. I might add, the rumblings of this distant thunder can be heard on a quiet night.

End of sermon.

In concluding the diatribe on this subject, there is only one true conclusion it's possible to reach. There's no finite answer to the opening question. There are entirely too many variables to be reckoned with.

Here are some questions you should ask yourself. Are the managed care patients you're about to take under your wing the type of patients you really want? Will your traditional patients be comfortable in a room full of the patients the managed care outfit or governmental entity sends you? Will Ms. Bigbucks walk out on you if she doesn't like what she sees in your waiting room? Sure, she's a prejudiced snob, but she pays her bills and sends you great referrals. Is signing up those extra bodies worth losing her and her friends?

Maybe so, but the question must be asked.

You must weigh your own attitudes and skills, your practice objectives, your limitations, the extent of managed care coverage in your area, your ability to convert a portion of those alternate care patients into traditional ones at times, the amount of free time you have on your hands, your office facility and a host of other considerations. Weigh them all before you decide.

Above all, don't panic. Remember the kiddie tale about Chicken Little. The sky isn't coming down in chunks.

# Chapter 18

# Structuring Fees And Analyzing Them For Profitability

Before we tackle this subject, I'd like to acknowledge the generosity of *DENTAL ECONOMICS*. Much of this chapter is lifted nearly verbatim from an article I wrote which appeared in the February 1994 issue. By allowing me to use the material, they've saved me a fair amount of grief in preparing this section, and I am extremely grateful.

Now, back to business. There's already been some discussion of fees previously, but only in generalities. Because fees are the basis for all profit or loss, you need to know what should go into determining a fair fee.

Having this information makes rational decisions regarding participation in alternative delivery methods possible. It makes setting fees in that first office a bit less scary. It makes taking apart that old fee schedule you're handed by a seller a logical process. It makes estimating what your competition's actually doing less of a guess.

History plays a big part in any dental fee schedule. We all know we're not operating in a vacuum. We have informal comparison shoppers galore who know not only what you're charging, but what the clinic down the street charges. The question then becomes, where did they get their fee schedule? Where did yours come from?

For the most part, the answer is, you both inherited it. And where did the guy you inherited it from get his? He inherited it, too! It's something like the old chicken and egg debate. Which came first? Who determined the original fees?

Since dentistry first became a profession, there has always been an informal "usual and customary" fee schedule for any community. It's an axiom that you should be reasonably competitive with your peers if you're to compete for the public dollar. Outside of a few renegades on either end of the fee scale, most dentists practicing in a trade area have always operated within a fairly narrow fee range.

Historically, when a new dentist came to town, he or she dug around and found out approximately what this community standard was and settled into it. The newcomer probably wasn't even aware most decisions regarding fees took place well before his or her birth.

For several generations, overhead ran somewhere in the neighborhood of 35 percent or less. With that kind of profit margin, there was a lot of room for error in the profit margin built into an individual fee. If you didn't make much of anything on one procedure or two, it didn't matter. You automatically made it up somewhere else. You could give discounts or do a fair amount of charity work and still make a good living.

There was far too little scientific basis for this old fee schedule. This was evidenced by the generally accepted benchmark for major items such as crowns, partials, and dentures. The saying went something to the effect that a fair fee for these services was three times the lab bill. On that basis it was comparatively simple to figure out what should be charged for other services.

There was an alternative called the Bosworth system. In the 1930s it became fairly popular to decide what you wanted to gross per hour and set your fees accordingly. Since overhead wasn't a major concern, there was always enough left over to provide a darned good living.

This crude management system had a lapsed-time clock as its centerpiece. You started it when you began to work and stopped it when you quit. If you were billing at the rate of $6 an hour, a fairly decent gross back then, you charged the patient 10 cents a minute. This sometimes led to some rather interesting fees, especially when you were charging $7.25 an hour.

The bookkeeping became a chore and many dentists soon developed a true fee schedule by averaging a number of individual fees for one procedure and rounding off those crazy odd-cent amounts to the nearest dollar or half-dollar. Only when the procedure was far more complex than the average did they alter the basic charge.

By 1950, fee schedules, whether developed by guess or by coin toss, had been institutionalized. There were even charts available which showed what you should charge in order to gross specific amounts per hour. Since overhead was so small, gross revenue was king.

Presto! Your present fee schedule was cast in stone! It's been adjusted for inflation. It's been adjusted—modestly—to reflect changes in efficiency. It's been adjusted to allow for differences in materials and technology. Nevertheless, it's still Gramps' old fees all dressed up in new duds. The much vaunted UCR and "percentile" lists are based on that outmoded time clock way of coming up with a fee.

Even the ADA helped perpetuate this method of doing business a few years ago. The ADA came up with a unit value rating system for common procedures. Simple extractions were one unit. If memory serves, three surface fillings were assigned a two-unit status.

The idea was, this could give insurance companies some yardstick when setting rates and fee allowances. The result was something similar to the diagnostically-related grouping method currently plaguing our medical brethren.

This outmoded fee scale determination wasn't too much of a problem until overhead started its upward creep. There was a lot of room for error when only a third of the money coming in went for keeping the doors open. As overhead rose and net income began to lag, dentists scrambled to increase productivity and efficiency to avoid pricing themselves out of business. It worked well for a time, but eventually overhead began to drag profits down again. When total average overhead topped 50 percent, we tried to make other adjustments to keep profits flowing.

One was to add the lab fee to a professional charge. Another was to start charging for items not formerly billed. Examples are cement bases, and prescriptions. It slowed the overhead drain slightly, but didn't cure the problem.

The result? We dentists started paying real attention to the way our offices were run. We began to look on dentistry as a business where a profit and loss statement means something. Yet, amazingly, we're still using a fee system that is as much as three-quarters of a century old and as outmoded as a Red Baron biplane.

Today it's considered normal to have an overhead of from 60 percent to 70 percent instead of the original 30 to 40 percent that dictated fees in earlier times. In some offices, overhead runs as high as 80 percent. It's easy to see the lack of any margin of error which allows for dips in production or unexpected expenses can wreak first class havoc in short order.

This makes understanding a fee structure and an overhead analysis crucial. It's downright critical when considering some proposal that demands a reduced total fee for any significant group of patients. Even the most uninitiated and naive practitioner immediately understands the concept that it's unwise to work highly skilled fingers clear through their latex gloves to produce a net loss.

Close scrutiny sometimes shows some fee-for-service charges are customarily provided at cost, or even below. The classic example is the ubiquitous prophy as cited in an earlier chapter. For most offices this is a "loss leader" unintentionally designed to keep patients coming back until they have a money-making problem.

With shrinking profit margins, most dentists want to make sure every procedure produces some sort of profit—even if it's a small one. Of course, if you don't know you're handing the equivalent of a crisp $5.00 bill to every patient who gets her teeth cleaned, you're not likely to make it a priority to raise that fee immediately.

Likewise, if you're establishing a fee schedule for the first time, you'll have a real justification for setting a fee at the high end of the "usual and customary" community standard. It's invaluable to know where your greatest profit is when, in order to be competitive, you're forced to abide by a pre-set competitive fee range.

So how do you determine a "fair" fee? It takes a bit of time to do the groundwork, but after that it becomes relatively easy. Follow along. I suggest you do your calculations for your requirements based on average monthly figures. If you're attempting this exercise for an office you're opening next month, there's a lot of guesswork involved. You'll have to make guesstimates of how long you'll take to do a procedure, how much it'll cost you, what your basic overhead will be, and other factors. Still, even that is better than striking out blindly ignorant.

You'll find it instructive to break your results down to what you'll have to produce every day to reach your income target. For some reason, this tends to take the figures out of the abstract category for most of us.

There are several components to any fee. There's basic overhead. That's what it costs you to keep your doors open whether or not anyone comes in. There's the cost of seeing a patient. Then there's another bit of overhead specific to doing any procedure. The final component is the hourly net wage you need to pay yourself to make it all worth the effort.

If you want to know how the analysis works, it's nuts and bolts time. Let's see how you arrive at what you *should* be charging based on the way a dental office operates today.

First, you need to answer two basic questions. One, how many hours are you actually productive? This is not the number of hours you're in the office.

It's how many hours you're actually dedicating to treating patients. There's a difference. In some offices, it's a very big difference.

If you're starting from scratch, I'd suggest you deduct about 25 percent from the hours you intend to work. You'll lose this much time taking care of nonproductive details. Once you've established a track record of efficiency, you can easily adjust your figures to fit your particular situation. If you've worked in someone else's office, use that experience as a guide. Just don't think you'll be 100 percent efficient.

If you're checking a practice that's for sale, hanging around a day or two will give you a good idea of the relative efficiency of the owner. You can then make adjustments to reflect how you would fare in the same setting.

The second question is how much money do you need to take home every month to ensure your life is rewarding and the practice a joy? Be honest with yourself. Ten million dollars a year would be grand, but realism demands practicality.

An honest answer to the first question may surprise you. It's amazing how many wasted hours we put in which can't, by any stretch, be called productive. All sorts of possibilities may suddenly present themselves for increasing efficiency and production. However, that's not the primary subject under discussion. It's merely an illuminating by-product of checking fees.

Once you have those two figures, it's no big task to figure how much you need to take in every productive hour for your own use. You simply divide the hours worked into the monthly requirement.

For instance, if you decide you want $5,000 a month, and you're working productively 100 hours a month, you need $50 an hour. This is the base for your fee schedule—your personal share of the patient's treatment dollar.

Keep this figure firmly fixed in your mind as you proceed. This is why you're getting up every morning. Without it, your commitment to dentistry can be considered nothing more than an expensive hobby.

Next, you need to total all the monthly fixed expenses you'll have. Things like rent, salaries, utilities, association dues, note payments, and taxes. These are the constant expenses that go on whether you have a patient or not. Total them and calculate the same sort of hourly figure arrived at in the example above. This is then added to your own "wage."

Let's divert from the main subject for a second. If you're relating these calculations to true overhead for purposes other than setting fees, you might want to pull your hourly wage out of the mix before you proceed.

While it's necessary when you're looking at a fee structure, you should leave it out when determining the viability of purchasing a practice. Neither should it be included when trying to figure what you'll end up with when joining a managed care scheme.

Don't forget the depreciation or amortization of your facility and equipment. These figures might not show up on a monthly balance sheet. Equally important, if you put in capital, you need to pay yourself interest on that money. Your investment should show some sort of return over and above your "salary."

The logical next progression is to find what the cost is to see a patient, whether or not there's a charge involved. You may think such expenses are incidental, but they do mount up. OSHA alone demands a continuing investment and cost to comply with all its regulations. In most practices, it currently takes from $3 to $5 to simply seat a patient. Things like masks, gloves, laundry, disposable towels, sterilizing necessities, and the like quickly assume significance.

You may also want to include in your seating charge such items as marketing and other odd expenses that don't seem to fit into any other category. You might be wise to include any of those small miscellaneous expenses like the toys you plan to give to kids when they've refrained from biting you.

You'll discover some gray areas. For example, if you'll be practicing in a building with a parking garage, you may pay a flat rate every month for your own car, plus a fee for each patient that uses the garage. Thus, parking can be a fixed or "seating" expense. Or both. I'd suggest breaking it down to allow you to understand where the money's going, and for what. Knowing where money goes is the first step to controlling expenses.

Once you have these base figures, you're ready to attack your actual fee schedule. Here, we borrow a page from the old Bosworth time system. You need to know about how long it takes to perform each procedure on your list.

Perhaps this last statement should be amended a bit. Obviously, not all class-two preparations are equal. That deep, broken down mess on the distal root of an upper second molar is much more stressful and time consuming than the tiny mesial spot in the contact point of a lower first bicuspid. Not only that, some patients squirm, some don't. Some patients gag. Some want to talk. Some even have to go to the bathroom every 10 minutes.

For now, settle for something approaching an average time. We'll deal with the variations later.

Even though you may be an experienced practitioner who's sure it takes precisely 20 minutes to do an average class two, check a few anyway.

Remember, we're basing fees on actual time spent, not on "goofing off" periods. Your appointment book may list something as a 30-minute procedure, but it may really be a 20- or 40-minute thing. It won't hurt to find out.

Here's a chance for a second by-product. If you're thorough in your investigation, you may become more conscious of where your time is going. This can lead to more efficient treatment planning.

Once you have the time factor, it's almost automatic to say you have the fee for a given treatment. It's simply a function of the hourly requirements you've already determined. Add to that the standard cost of seating the patient in the chair, and you have it. Almost.

To this must be added the specific cost of the individual treatment. You've used up a bur or two on that prep. There was anesthesia, needle and all. Then there's the filling material. Or the lab bill. Or the polishing paste. True, this may vary from fifty cents to hundreds of dollars, but each cost should be factored. It all adds up.

Now you have the true fee you should be charging.

There are several discretionary areas you might consider in your final fee determination. The first is treatment planning and consultation time. In the scenario just set forth, these are not considered productive times, and therefore not charged for. If the patient actually accepts treatment, the time is made up for by the fee charged.

In the event a considerable number of patients refuse your treatment plan, a charge might be calculated for your wasted effort. This approach may also be useful in special practice situations where the diagnosis is what the patient is after, rather than some potential treatment.

The difficult patient, or the difficult treatment may be addressed by merely adding a given percentage to the standard fee. Alternatively, the five minute pit cavity might be worthy of a discount. This becomes a matter of judgment, and must be determined by the individual situation. If you vary your fees, at least you'll be aware of what you're doing and your decision will be based on facts.

A second arbitrary decision may come when you spend time away from the operatory on the patient's behalf as a part of treatment. This may include surveying models for partial dentures, pouring delicate impressions, or marking dies. Including this time in the final fee is a matter of judgment. If you charge for it, you should include it in your hourly total of time spent in treating patients.

You may also want to include a provision for redoing your work.

Nobody's perfect. Sometimes, through no discernible fault of yours, that beautiful bridge isn't satisfactory and must be replaced in a couple of months. You might want to set up some sort of reserve for those unhappy occurrences. If so, tack it on your fees.

Though it may seem minor, there's the cost of record keeping, mailing bills, and handling insurance forms. It might be prudent to include a small charge in each fee for these miscellaneous items. Alternatively, you could include them in the fixed expense category, or the patient seating charge.

A word of warning. Determining a fee schedule using this method is a time consuming task. Getting the data sorted out is not fun. Take heart. It doesn't have to be done every time you adjust your fees. Three or four times throughout your career should be adequate to provide a firm base for adjusting your charges unless you feel a problem is creeping into your office.

There are variations of this method you can use if you wish. It's possible to arrive at an approximation of a cost-based fee by taking the total expense of your office over a given period and applying it equally to procedures without regard to individual treatment costs.

When the hourly profit you wish is added, you have a rough idea of what your fees should be. Then add any major specific cost, such as lab charges. However, this is not nearly as accurate as going step by step. Nor does it point out faults in your practice nearly as well.

A word of warning. Once you do all of this calculating and compare the results to the prevailing fee structures in your area, you're liable to find the ideal fee isn't particularly valid for the world you live in. You'll have to use common sense and compromise in attempting to implement such a radical fee structure.

For example, you'd undoubtedly charge a far larger fee for a four-unit bridge than you would for two single crowns. Most dentists I know charge about twice as much. The chances are you'll discover the bridge can be placed for a couple of hundred dollars more than the crowns. While you might be willing to adjust your fee downward somewhat, there's no way you'll cut it that far.

Likewise, if you intend doing your own prophys, you'll never be able to adequately recoup your real cost. To do so would price you right out of the market. What this particular analysis will do is help you make a decision whether or not it might be worthwhile to hire a hygienist. Or conversely, to fire the one that's in the office you're buying. That would make sense if she's costing more than you'd lose doing the work yourself.

Perhaps the biggest advantage to knowing exactly what each procedure is worth is in deciding whether or not to join a particular alternative health plan. I know you're getting tired of hearing me repeat it, but evaluating a scheme becomes much easier when you know precisely how and where you must cut expenses, or your profit, if you sign up. Not knowing can be expensive!

For example, I recall analyzing a practice a couple of years ago where the dentist was, amazingly, losing money with a gross approaching $200,000. Fee-for-service patients were providing him with half his gross, and were netting him nearly $40,000. His PPO and capitation patients were contributing the other $100,000 gross, but his expense in treating them was nearly $130,000! Until he sat down and looked at the figures, he couldn't understand why his net was shrinking while his gross kept ballooning.

To any experienced practitioner, implementing the fee schedule developed by this method will not look feasible at all. In our real world, our fees are most often determined by those of our colleagues. Nevertheless, there are massive management advantages to trying this exercise.

One obvious business advantage is the possibility of eliminating, as much as possible, unprofitable services from your repertoire. If your fee for extractions should be $50, but the community going rate is only $25, you might be wise to refer as many as you can to an oral surgeon.

Alternatively, you could emphasize a particular service where you'll net more money than your costs require. You might even find it profitable to cut that fee somewhat as an inducement to patients to accept a higher level of treatment.

The varied uses for the cost analysis part of this fee determination are nearly endless. The information is crucial if you plan to hire an associate, add or eliminate staff members, offer a new technique, or install an expensive piece of equipment. It will allow you to find out exactly how profitable it would be to share space with another practitioner or to form a partnership of some sort.

As mentioned earlier, simply going through the exercise may point out problem areas in production and efficiency.

Even if you don't end up making a single change in your community's average fee schedule, at least you'll know where the money's coming from, and precisely where it's going. That's an invaluable bit of wisdom to possess in the uncertain times ahead.

# Chapter 19

# A Checklist

Here's a list of some of the things you must attend to before you open that new office. It's not all inclusive. Neither is the list in strict chronological order. Your individual situation may require additions and alterations of the order in which each task is accomplished. Use it only as a guide and memory prompter.

1. Be sure you're personally ready to assume the burdens of private practice. Make sure both your professional and management skills are adequate for the task.

2. Decide on a general location and arrange for licensure in your desired area.

3. Develop your practice plans, including aims and goals. Incorporate these into an interim office manual.

4. Begin your location search. If contemplating buying a practice, contact a broker.

5. Narrow location search.

6. Learn what local and state restrictions and regulations will apply to the area you've focused on. This includes such items as building codes, advertising restrictions, special taxes, and more.

7. Update any data you have concerning your personal financial history and make initial contact with potential lenders.

8. If buying a practice, make initial contact with seller and, if favorable, begin assessment of the practice.

9. Alternatively, locate office space and begin negotiations for occupancy. When satisfied, sign lease or purchase agreement. If buying or building, begin coordination of architects, real estate people, builders, and other interested parties.

10. Make a decision on the type and extent of equipment you'll need.

11. Prepare a loan proposal and obtain financing.

12. Check with the phone company to see when phone books are published. If necessary, arrange for phone listing early to avoid missing the deadline.

13. If buying a practice, complete the assessment and begin negotiations, including any loan arrangements.

14. Contact your attorney and accountant to check any paperwork that's come up by this stage. Do this before signing anything.

15. Decide on a contractor to do remodeling or construction.

16. If buying a practice, complete negotiations and have attorneys begin transfer of papers.

17. Begin initial external marketing.

18. *Closely* supervise any construction and remodeling.

19. Arrange for all insurance.

20. Join professional and civic organizations.

21. Purchase furniture for waiting room and arrange for delayed delivery.

22. Purchase office supplies and equipment. Order paper goods, including stationery.

23. If required, update office manual.

24. Interview potential ancillary personnel. Make decisions about who to hire.

25. Obtain any remaining permits and licenses needed to open your door. Check with your accountant for instructions about complying with tax and other financial regulatory requirements.

26. Prepare announcements and other advertising to commence on opening date.

27. Purchase any unordered drugs and supplies.

28. Coordinate delivery and installation of all equipment and furnishings.

29. Arrange for remaining utility installation.

30. Arrange for cleanup after all workmen have departed. Engage janitorial service if desired.

31. Double check the functioning of all equipment before opening for business. Double check to see all needed supplies are in stock on the premises.

32. Have in-depth meetings with all assistants to ensure complete understanding of how the office is to be run. Have each read and initial the office manual. Meet both individually and as a group to iron out potential difficulties.

33. Review everything.

34. If buying a practice, sign the final papers.

35. Secure releases and receipts from all contractors, subcontractors, construction consultants, and others to prevent future liability for bills they might not have paid.

36. Implement marketing plan fully.

I am sorely tempted to add a final item to the checklist admonishing you to check with your physician to see if you've developed an ulcer. This will be one of the most stressful times in your life. Take time out along the way for a deep breath and some relaxation.

Again, this list is not complete, nor does it cover all situations. Sorry, it simply can't. There are too many variables. You'll add to it as you go along. The trick is to be organized and anticipate problems so you can behead them before they become crises.

# Chapter 20

# Conclusions

In a book of this sort it hardly seems necessary to sum up or distill out essentials for a final examination. Nevertheless, it won't hurt to repeat one last time the big message I've tried to impart.

In case you haven't already had it drummed into your head, here it is: Opening that first office is one of the most, if not the most, important series of decisions you'll make in your adult life. It ranks right up there with marriage and well ahead of where to go on your next vacation. It therefore deserves a considerable investment in thought, time and money.

That last may be a sore point with the newer dentist whose resources are limited. Spending a few dollars up front may mean the inability to buy a coveted bit of equipment for that new office. It might mean not purchasing that prize practice on the spot. Nonetheless, it will be money well spent over the long haul.

Carve it in the top of your desk: "Look before you leap!" It's a cliche', and therefore scorned in literary circles. The truth is, old sayings stick around because they carry an abiding nugget of wisdom. This one most definitely does. If you've gleaned nothing else from this book but that axiom, then you've received your money's worth.

One last drop of advice to fill your cup. There is a small list of books for recommended reading in the appendix section. Take them to heart. Study them. Each covers in detail a specific section of the practice of dentistry. Each will contribute materially to your income over the next few years and make your dental practice much more enjoyable.

I make no apologies for the fact that many, if not most, of these books come from the same publisher as this one. They're written for the practitioner who has wet gloves and spattered gown, generally by practitioners who've been down the same road you're traveling. Others are penned by experts who've analyzed more offices than you'll ever visit. Profit from their wisdom, and sometimes from their admitted mistakes.

Finally, at long last, I wish you well as you venture into the tangled world of private practice. May you prosper both financially and personally!

# APPENDIX 1

# BASIC DATA NEEDED TO ANALYZE A PRACTICE

## PRODUCTION

The following main calculations are necessary to understand the actual production and possible production potential of an office. By manipulating these figures in various ways you can determine such things as office production, dentist's production, wasted time, and more.

1. Determine the percentage of gross production created by alternative delivery contracts.

2. Divide gross production by actual hours worked to obtain ideal hourly charge.

3. Adjust for downtime in the office to arrive at potential gross.

4. Adjust this figure to meet your own production skills to determine your own potential production potential in the office.

5. Calculate the collection percentage by comparing the gross production with gross receipts.

6. Determine the percentage of production produced by someone other than the dentist, for example, hygienists.

Here are two examples of how this information can be used. Use your own ingenuity to manipulate the figures for your own needs.

## EXAMPLE 1

Production total_____

Divided by hours worked_____

Equals hourly gross charge_____

## EXAMPLE 2

Monthly gross receipts_____

Less percentage loss of production
as a result of change of ownership_____

Less total overhead_____

Equals amount available for servicing debt_____

*Appendix 1*

# FEES

Here are the calculations outlined in the chapter on fees. They are also valuable in determining numerous other aspects of a practice you're thinking of buying.

**OVERHEAD:**
These are the items that usually comprise fixed overhead:

1. Telephone_____

2. Rent or mortgage_____

3. Taxes, all types_____

4. Salaries, including pension plans, FICA, etc._____

5. Insurance, all types_____

6. Utilities_____

7. Contract advertising_____

8. Payments on equipment_____

9. Civic and professional dues_____

10. Consulting fees (accountant, etc.)_____

11. Note payments_____

12. Return on capital investment_____

13. Depreciation_____

**Total**_____

**Total divided by hours worked per month**_____

**PROCEDURE COST**

*Example: Single crown.*

    Prep costs: burs, stones, anesthesia, etc_____

    Impression costs: material, disposable tray,
    stone, mailing cost, etc_____

    Lab fee_____

    Insertion costs: cement, glazing, finishing
    materials, etc_____

        Subtotal_____

        *Seating cost per visit, X number of visits
        for procedure_____

        **Total**_____

*Seating cost includes all disposables required to see a patient whether work is performed or not. Includes sterilization, cleanup, OSHA mandates, bibs, gowns, tissues, and other suitable items.

*Appendix 1*

**FINAL FEE DETERMINATION**

    Hourly basic requirement_____

    Plus total hourly fixed overhead_____

        Subtotal_____

    X hours (or fraction of hours) procedure requires

        Subtotal_____

        Plus direct cost of procedure_____

        **Actual fair fee for procedure**_____

## Consultants

There are two categories of consultants you will probably need to call on in certain situations when you enter private practice. The earlier you engage them, the better you'll be able to coordinate your project. Be sure to pick people you're comfortable with and feel you can trust. If possible, interview a number of individuals. If you happen to like a particular company but cannot connect with the individual you're supposed to work with, ask for a replacement. It's your money.

**Primary**

In any office situation you'll always need the services of the following people to some extent. Because the relationship with these people will undoubtedly be long-term, take extra care in your selection.

1. Attorney

2. Accountant (May also serve as estate planner or provide other financial advice above and beyond purely actuarial data)

3. Insurance agent and advisor (May also provide similar financial advice to that listed for accountants)

**Secondary**

The following consultants are available if you feel the necessity. In certain situations, one or more may be critical. In others, that same individual might not be required as a consultant or even as an informal advisor. Some of these relationships may also turn into long-term associations.

1. Banker

2. General contractor

3. Architect

4. Building inspector

5. Color consultant

6. Lighting engineer

*Appendix 1*

7. Appraisers:
   a. Real Estate
   b. Equipment
   C. Practice

8. Real estate agent

9. Management consultant

10. Employment agency

11. Advertising agency

12. Marketing consultant

13. Mortgage broker

# APPENDIX 2

# QUESTIONS TO ASK YOURSELF

## SHOULD YOU BE IN PRIVATE PRACTICE?

Here are a number of thought-provoking questions, in addition to those posed in the text, that you'd do well to consider before you step out into private practice. They're intended to supplement the issues and problems in the foregoing chapters. Though they're listed to roughly correlate with the various subjects discussed, please consider them in the overall context of opening or buying a private practice rather then merely the narrow confines of their particular subjects.

Please be aware there are no "correct" answers. A valid solution for you in your planned practice might not be appropriate for any of your dental school classmates. The sole purpose of these brain-nudgers is to make you think. Possibly they'll give you a framework for discussion with your peers.

Because they fit in so well, here are the questions asked in chapter 1 to help determine if you're suited for private solo practice. They should also help you determine what type of practice is best suited for you. They're repeated here to provide a base for the other brain exercisers.

1. Are you cut out to handle a large volume of patients or are you better off with a smaller, more intimate operation?

2. Do you want a traditional fee-for-service arrangement, or can you be successful contracting with one or more HMO or other alphabet alternative modalities?

3. What type of patient are you most comfortable with?

4. Will you be miserable if you must compromise even one professional standard you've set for yourself?

5. Can you honestly say you're the type who can be the boss, understanding all that the term implies?

6. Can you manage employees?

7. Can you manage money?

8. Do you understand all the legal responsibilities and restrictions owning a business places on you?

9. Do you have the personality traits that are needed to run a successful practice?

10. If you're not the traditional public's stereotype of professional (e.g., female, minority, handicapped, etc.), have you weighed this factor into your decision?

These additional bits of cogitational goulash are not necessarily covered specifically in the text.

1. What management skills are most important for a successful private solo practice?

2. What management skills are most important in a group practice or partnership?

3. What personal personality traits are most desirable for a successful solo practice?

4. What personal traits are best for successful participation in a group practice or partnership?

5. To what extent will a lack of one or more of these traits inhibit financial success in each setting?

6. To what extent do *any* personality traits influence success in different practice types or locations?

7. What is your definition of financial success?

8. Does achieving financial success conflict with your personal concept of happiness?

9. What personal goals do you have that might affect your financial and professional decisions and goals?

10. To what extent do the ethics of the profession inhibit or enhance the attainment of your financial goals?

11. Will the attainment of professional goals require personal sacrifices, and are you comfortable with those sacrifices?

12. To what extent will strictly personal considerations influence your decisions regarding your future choices in the manner in which you practice dentistry?

13. Besides obvious immediate financial requirements, what are the advantages to working in a salaried position initially?

14. What are the disadvantages?

15. What do you consider the optimum time frame for salaried employment and why?

16. What are the advantages of choosing an alternative career?

17. What are the disadvantages?

18. What personal and psychological attributes are desirable in these alternative careers?

19. In establishing long-term plans and goals, what do you consider "long term?"

20. How far ahead should you plan when establishing an office?

21. What do you feel is an adequate time to allow for both planning and execution of that plan when opening an office?

22. What conditions exert the most influence on that time frame?

23. What patient needs do you feel are not being currently addressed by the profession that would provide an opportunity for the beginner to more quickly establish a practice?

24. Would serving those unfullfilled needs ultimately limit the overall scope and success of a practice?

25. Would any of these alternative approaches or treatments be cost effective in dealing with managed care patients?

26. What changes in the next five years (other than technical) do you envision that will impact the manner in which dentistry is delivered to the patient? How about in 10 years or 20 years?

27. To what extent should you plan for these changes when setting up a practice?

28. New treatments, delivery concepts, and other ideas are constantly being offered to the profession. Most fall by the wayside as nothing more than fads. What criteria should you have for measuring the worth of these new approaches before incorporating them into your practice?

## LOCATION

1. What do you consider the prime factors influencing the selection of a general location for a practice?

2. What factors are least important?

3. How are these factors altered when purchasing an existing practice?

*Appendix 2*

4. Should these factors be considered when joining an existing practice or group?

5. To what extent should purely personal and family considerations influence a choice of location?

6. Does the fact that those considerations may be immediate or future possibilities have a greater bearing on that choice?

7. How do marketing strategies affect a choice of location—and vice versa?

8. To what extent should you allow availability of initial financing to influence your choice of location?

9. What type of location would prove least expensive in which to open an office?

10. What type of location would be the most expensive?

11. What locations, though ultimately desirable, would prove the most difficult in which to initially establish a profitable practice?

12. What do you consider the minimum space in which to open an office?

13. To what extent does the type of practice influence that answer?

14. How much expansion room should you allow for when choosing an office location?

15. To what extent does the office location affect the fees; office hours; participation in alternative managed care arrangements; type and emphasis of treatment offered and delivered to patients; type and extent of advertising and other external marketing; office design, layout and furnishings; equipment installed; type of patients the office will attract; and patient acceptance of treatment proposals.

16. To what extent will each of the above impact either positively or negatively on a potential patient pool?

17. All location choices require compromises. What compromises will have the most impact on practice potential?

18. In buying a practice, how important is the location, and how much is it worth?

19. To what extent does choice of location affect long-term goals?

20. What strategies can you come up with to make a basically undesirable location work in your favor?

21. A chauvinistic question—in the practical real world, do age, sex, or racial characteristics influence a dentist's choice of location? If so, why? If not, why not?

22. What do you feel is a reasonable time to allow for finding office space?

23. If you're unable to find the exact office space you need in your selected location, to what extent should you compromise? Would it be better to postpone your plans for a while?

24. What are the economic advantages and disadvantages of opening multiple offices or a satellite office?

25. How does this possibility apply differently to a specialist as opposed to a general practitioner?

26. Second offices cost additional money to maintain. What can be done to compensate for the additional overhead?

**SCOPING OUT YOUR COMPETITION**

1. In each of the various office settings described— urban, suburban and rural—how far away must a colleague's office be before he or she ceases to be serious competition for the patient pool you're after?

*Appendix 2*

2. What factors go into determining if an area already has enough practitioners?

3. Even if an area is apparently adequately covered by others, what factors might make it possible for you to make a living there?

4. How can you determine if a portion of the patient pool in an area is underserved or ignored by existing practitioners?

5. How would you go about gauging the satisfaction of a potential patient pool in its present dental treatment?

6. Do you think a patient pool's utilization of physicians has any correlation to the utilization of dentists? Why or why not?

7. If you discover an underserved group of patients in an otherwise adequately-served area and gear your practice toward attracting these patients, to what extent do you think the other dentists in the area will expand their own practices to go into direct competition with you?

8. What niches do you think your competitors will cede to you without a struggle?

9. If you join a group practice in any capacity, under what conditions do you think the other members of the group might turn out to be underhanded competition?

10. Will your possible future status with the group have an effect on that answer?

11. To what extent do you think ethical professional standards might be compromised in an overserved area?
12. If you find yourself in such an area, to what extent would you be willing to compromise your own ethical standards to make a living?

## BUY, BUILD OR LEASE

1. What are the relative economic advantages in owning your own facility?

2. What are the economic disadvantages and long-term liabilities?

3. What determines the break-even point between the two?

4. Economics aside, what are the other advantages and disadvantages to owning versus renting?

5. How does the practice type affect these answers?

6. When buying or negotiating a lease/purchase agreement, what is better long term, a higher initial sales price with a low interest rate or a lower selling price with a high interest rate? Why?

7. In a lease/purchase arrangement, should the sales price be linked to the length of the lease?

8. What would you consider a reasonable time limit on such a lease and how renewable should it reasonably be?

9. In this situation, sometimes a portion of the lease payment is applied as a down payment. How should this affect the lease arrangements?

10. How does the length of a proposed mortgage built into the lease affect this situation?

11. Are the same answers valid for both the beginning and the established dentist?

12. What factors should be checked beyond zoning, location, and clear title when buying land on which to construct an office?

13. Do these considerations apply with equal force to buying a building for remodeling?

*Appendix 2*

14. If you buy or build, how long must you remain in that location for it to be financially advantageous when compared to leasing comparable quarters?

15. What variables connected with practice demographics will have an effect on your answer?

16. What factors other than practice considerations will affect that answer?

17. To what extent should those other considerations enter into your decision?

18. What neighboring businesses will most enhance a practice?

19. What businesses might detract from it?

20. What businesses would not affect it?

21. How will the type of practice you intend to conduct affect the answers to those last questions?

22. How are those answers influenced by the character of the location such as part ownership of each of the following: office building, mall, strip center, free standing facility, or other.

23. Is this answer equally valid for urban, suburban, and rural settings?

24. Successful practices have been developed in each of the following unusual locations. How do these nontraditional facilities lend themselves to marketing a practice? Would you be interested in an old fire station, an abandoned filling station, a railway coach, an old barn or carriage house, or an ante-bellum home.

25. How would each possibly inhibit attracting the widest possible patient pool?

26. Would the additional expense of attempting to maintain as much of the original flavor of such a nontraditional site be cost effective in attracting patients?

27. Do such unusual locations lend themselves more to general practice or to a specialty?

28. How do such sites lend themselves to unusual marketing possibilities?

29. Under what conditions would constructing a new facility to imitate one of these unusual buildings enhance or detract from a practice?

30. What types of practice would most benefit from utilization of such a building?

## FINANCING

1. What is the most creative financing package you can think of to minimize a down payment on a practice purchase?

2. Which, if any, of these strategies could be applied to starting a practice?

3. What additional financial hazards would such a creative scheme create?

4. What percentage of the total capital required to open an office do you feel the beginner should have?

5. Will this figure vary according to the amount of experience the dentist has in private practice? If so, to what extent?

6. What do you feel is the minimum net worth a lending institution will need to see on a loan application before they'll seriously consider a loan for either opening or buying a dental office?

7. How about buying into a group or partnership?

8. What is your estimate of how long it would take to process a loan application for financing a dental office?

9. What do you think the maximum amount of time would be allowed for repayment of that loan?

*Appendix 2*

10. Again, would the amount of experience the borrower has in private practice influence this decision?

11. What do you feel a dentist must gross in order to meet his or her continuing basic overhead?

12. How long do you think it would take the average dentist opening his or her first office to reach that break-even point?

13. To what extent will a partnership, group practice or space-sharing arrangement affect this figure?

14. How would one of these arrangements affect the viability of a loan request?

15. What are the overall financing advantages and disadvantages of leasing equipment?

16. What are the advantages and disadvantages of financing a facility and a practice separately?

17. Should the two be financed with different institutions or lenders?

18. If you extend credit to patients, what methods are available to control bad debts?

19. What alternatives are there to offering credit without limiting your patient's ability to pay for treatment?

20. In extending credit, what percentage of your annual gross should be in the form of payment plans?

21. If you extend credit, should you charge interest?

22. What perils, above and beyond bad debts, do you face if you do?

23. In any practice it takes time to achieve profitability. How should you finance this interim shortfall?

24. How much time should you reasonably allow in planning for this shortfall? Why?

25. How could you use extending credit to patients as an asset to improve your credit line with a bank?

## PURCHASING A PRACTICE

1. It usually costs more initially to purchase a practice than it does to open an office on your own. At what point does either strategy become more cost effective than the other?

2. What nonfinancial factors influence such a choice?

3. When buying a practice outright, what do you feel is an acceptable percentage of the price you would need as a down payment? Why?

4. How will other terms of the sale affect this?

5. How long should the selling doctor remain to introduce the new owner, and at what point does his or her presence become a liability?

6. What factors influence this decision?

7. To what extent does this answer influence the answer to the next question, and vice versa?

8. To what extent does patient loyalty to a selling dentist influence the value of a practice?

9. Under what circumstances can that patient loyalty be a liability?

10. What marketing strategies should a buyer employ to enhance patient transfer?

11. What marketing strategies would be counterproductive?

12. How long should you allow for negotiations when buying a practice?

13. Under what circumstances should you hire your own consultant when buying a practice?

14. What are the greatest hazards to look out for in buying a practice?

15. When you buy a practice, you'll want to make changes. What changes can be made fairly rapidly? What changes should *not* be made for some time? Why?

16. What marketing strategies can you use after you buy a practice to attract new patients without chasing off the old ones?

17. If a selling dentist remains in the practice as an associate, what is the best method of compensating him or her?

18. Should you pay him/her a premium for any name value brought to the arrangement? If so, under what circumstances?

19. Sometimes a young dentist who can't make it will offer a practice for sale. Under what circumstances, if any, should you consider buying such a practice?

20. Does the introduction of a temporary dentist into a practice that's been closed have a positive or negative effect?

21. What are the conditions that influence that effect?

22. What factors influence the amount of time it takes for a closed practice to lose its value?

23. How long do you think it takes for a practice to lose its goodwill when the office doors are closed? What factors will retard or accelerate the process?

24. What marketing strategies may be employed to recapture those patients?

## PARTNERSHIPS AND GROUPS

1. When buying into a group practice after serving as an associate, is the seller justified in asking for cash? Why?

2. What are the hazards of forming an immediate partnership with someone who is currently operating a solo practice?

3. What financing advantages are there to buying into a group or partnership as opposed to a straight buyout of a solo practice?

4. What are the other advantages and disadvantages?

5. What strategies should be employed to protect members of a group from the actions of another member of that group?

6. What do you see as the principal hazards of buying into the corporate structure of a group?

7. What are the advantages?

8. What are the advantages and disadvantages of forming a partnership to jointly hold the tangible assets of a facility while each member maintains a distinct solo practice?

9. How much professional freedom do you think you would give up when joining a group practice?

10. How do you minimize this?

11. How would you go about building up a loyal following for you personally within a group structure?

12. How would this differ from what could be done in a solo practice?

13. In a group, should you be compensated strictly on the basis of the group's total profitability or should you receive additional compensation for your own efforts?

*Appendix 2*

14. If you feel you should be compensated additionally, should this additional compensation be linked to the percentage of the group structure you own?

15. Assuming you have the financial resources (or can borrow the money) to do so, is it better to buy into a group in incremental stages until you attain a full and equal status, or should you buy that status all at once? Why?

16. When buying into a group, you're making a sizeable investment. How do you determine a fair rate of return on that investment?

17. Should that return start immediately, should it be deferred until later, or a combination of the two? Why?

18. What economies in overhead can be achieved in a group practice or partnership?

19. What additional expenses are there?

## SPACE SHARING

Some of the following questions concern matters that are best discussed with competent legal counsel. They're included to start you thinking about the many ramifications that can occur in what is, on the surface, a simple arrangement. I suggest you use them as a springboard to looking for other situations that might complicate things between the parties involved.

1. What is the single biggest advantage to space sharing?

2. What is the single biggest disadvantage?

3. If you're leasing from another dentist in a space-sharing situation, what percentage of the total overhead should you pay?

4. What factors influence this percentage?

5. If you're the lessee and something breaks while it's your turn in the office, should you be responsible? If so, to what extent?

6. What determines how much, if any, office hours can overlap?

7. What ethical problems can arise between the doctors involved in a space-sharing environment?

8. Lawsuits are all too common. What protection do you need to avoid being a party to a suit because of your space-sharing buddy making a mistake?

9. What form should this protection take?

10. Obviously, in a space-sharing arrangement, both parties should maintain separate malpractice coverage. Should the lessee rely on the prime dentist's general liability policy, should they both purchase separate policies, or should they obtain one joint policy? Why?

11. Would a joint policy create some sort of partnership, thus increasing the liability of each party?

12. Why would a space-sharing arrangement be a desirable prelude to forming a partnership?

13. Patients often become accustomed to going to a particular location for treatment as a matter of convenience or habit. If you lease space and later leave, what measures can you take to ensure your patients stick with you instead of transferring to your former roommate?

14. How do you prevent your former roommate from actively soliciting your patients?

15. Do you have any recourse if he or she does?

16. Such an action is undoubtedly unethical. Do you think it's illegal as well?

17. How does participation in certain managed care plans affect space sharing arrangements?

18. How do different practice goals, treatment emphasis, and philosophies of the sharing parties affect their business relationship?

19. How do they affect their individual practices?

20. To avoid internal and external conflict, should such things as fee schedules and salaries be similar?

## MANAGED CARE

1. What do you feel is an acceptable proportion of managed care patients in a private practice?

2. Does this percentage apply equally to solo and partnership or group practices?

3. To what extent do the location and type of practice influence this opinion?

4. Is this percentage the same for both HMO and PPO plans?

5. It's possible for a dentist to manage the utilization rate for managed care patients. What strategies are employed for this?

6. What impact does this have on professional ethics?

7. Does utilization control impact HMO and PPO patients differently? Why?

8. What is to be gained in controlling utilization by PPO patients?

9. Which creates the greater impact on the fee-for-service portion of a private practice, HMO contracts, or PPO contracts?

10. If you comingle PPO patients with fee-for-service patients, how do you justify the lower fees of the PPO group to the fee-for-service bunch?

11. What factors within the dental community are pushing the profession toward managed care? Why?

12. What factors, other than those listed in the text, are inhibiting the growth of dental managed care? Why?

13. In setting up an office, how does the planned inclusion of managed care patients affect the physical layout of an office?

14. Is additional equipment required to successfully participate in a managed care program? If so, what?

15. What additional personnel might be required to operate a practice that relies heavily on managed care contracts? Why?

16. In a managed care contract that offers only minimal profit directly, what strategies can you come up with that will turn enough of these patients into temporary fee-for-service patients to make the contract worthwhile?

17. Should you raise your general fee structure in a mixed practice to make up for any shortfall in managed care delivery?

18. Would such a move be ethical?

19. Would it be ethical to have two fee schedules; one for regular fee-for-service patients and another higher one for managed care patients who opt for specific fee-for-service treatment to make up for the bargain they've been receiving?

20. Ethics and morals aside, would such a strategy be legal?
21. Most outsiders view managed care concepts as being the same for medicine and dentistry. There are, however, significant differences. What are these differences? How can they be utilized for additional profitability in a contract? Which differences have a negative impact on dental delivery?

22. Other than those mentioned in the text, what additional liabilities are you facing when treating managed care patients?

## FEES

1. What do you consider a reasonable hourly charge for your expertise?

*Appendix 2*

2. Should this figure change as you gain experience?

3. How is this figure affected by the location and patient mix of the practice?

4. In the various types of locations described, what alterations should be made in a fee schedule to make the practice more attractive to patients?

5. What is the effect of any fee schedule on a patient's perception of the quality of care being delivered?

6. What do you think is an acceptable ratio of gross to net in a practice?

7. How much difference do group, partnership, and space-sharing arrangements make on this figure?

8. To what extent does the patient load have an effect on the fees charged?

9. What effect does this have on the fee schedule you originally adopt?

10. What factors influence how often a fee schedule should be changed?

11. Should that change be a general one for all fees, or just for part of them?

12. To what extent does the type of marketing employed influence the fee schedule of an office?

13. In a group practice, should the fee schedule be uniform for all members of the group? Why?

14. Do you feel patients are attracted to an office because of the fee schedule, and what bearing does it have on their retention?

15. What type of patients are most attracted by low fees? High fees?

16. Does a fee schedule have any significant bearing on the retention of HMO or PPO patients?

17. If you offer nontraditional hours, should there be a differential between the fee schedule used in those alternate hours as opposed to what are considered normal hours?

18. What should fee increases be linked to: overhead, community fee adjustments, general inflation, relative professional skill, or other factors?

19. What effect do surveys and UCR tables have on fee structures and fee increases?

20. Should fee schedules be the same for cash patients as for those who need a payment plan? Why?

21. To whom and under what circumstances should you discount fees?

22. In presenting a patient with a treatment plan, how much of a cushion should you put into the fee quoted to allow for unforseen difficulties?

23. Should you tell the patient about the cushion? Why, or why not?

24. If no difficulties occur, should you then lower the fee?

25. You try to sell a patient a four-unit bridge and are unsuccessful. Later, as the patient comes in for other treatment, your assistant convinces that patient of the necessity of the bridge. Should you give the assistant a commission?

26. Is such a commission legal? Is it ethical?

27. How does such a commission differ from the fairly common practice of offering the help a profit-sharing arrangement or a bonus when the office reaches a target goal of production or gross?

28. How can a fee schedule be slanted to assist in reaching such targets?

29. How much of a temptation do such goals present both doctor and staff to oversell unneeded treatment to reach those goals?

*Appendix 2*

## CONSULTANT LIST

1. What functions do you think the primary consultants listed should play in developing your plans for your office?

2. How do their roles differ in setting up an office on your own, buying an office outright, entering a group or partnership, or entering a space-sharing situation?

3. In hiring each of the primary consultants and advisors, what attributes and experience should you look for in each of the above situations?

4. Are these the same qualities you should look for in each advisor after you're in practice? Why or why not?

5. What are the most important insurance policies for you to buy? What are the least important? Why?

6. To what extent should the cost of each type of insurance influence your decision to purchase or only buy limited coverage of a particular policy?

7. What cost-cutting strategies could you employ to expand your overall coverage or increase the limits of the individual policies?

8. Everyone has friends, friends of the family, relatives, classmates, or neighbors who make their living in one or more of the areas listed. What are the advantages and disadvantages of using one or more of these people as a consultant?

9. How does the individual field of expertise of the person under discussion influence this decision?

10. In which of the many practice settings and types would each of the secondary consultants prove most helpful? Least helpful?

11. With each of the consultants listed, to what extent should you turn decision making over to the consultant?

12. Even if you have confidence in your consultant, under what circumstances should you look for a second opinion?

13. When you call an employment agency or place an ad in the local paper, what qualifications do you think are most important in hiring any assistant? How do these differ for the various positions that may be required in your office?

14. Do these qualifications vary depending upon the practice type? In what way? Does office location have a bearing?

15. How are these qualifications different for the new practitioner than for the established one?

16. Some management consultants offer a wide variety of individualized services. Others limit their talents to a narrow aspect of practice management, thus requiring the services of several outfits from time to time. Still others offer a standardized approach where their advice and management in all the offices they service is the same, thus offering a less expensive alternative. In which practice situation is each type the most cost effective?

17. Under what circumstances and to what extent do you think a management consultant can serve as a substitute for some of the other possible consultants on the list?

# APPENDIX 3

# USEFUL ADDITIONAL READING

1. Combs, Ron. *Dental Economics Office Design Ideas.* Tulsa: PennWell Publishing Co., 1995.

2. Lacey, Dan, *The Paycheck Disruption.* Hippocrene Books, 1988.

3. Layman, George, D.D.S., and Jack Powers. *Dental Office Planning: Conception to Occupancy.* Tulsa: PennWell Publishing Co., 1982.

4. Levoy, Bob. *How to Hire, Keep, and Motivate Top-Notch Employees.* Roslyn, New York: Success Dynamics, Inc., 1991. Six cassette tapes.

5. Mayes, Donald S. *Managed Dental Care: a Guide to Dental HMOs.* Brookfield, Wisconsin: International Foundation of Employee Benefit Plans, 1993.

6. Palmer, Diane M., M.B.A., and Shrise Hanna, B.S., *The Telephone Handbook for Medical and Dental Practices.* Aurora, Illinois: Palmer Associates, Inc., 1989.

7. Powers, Jack, and George Layman, *D.D.S. Dental Office Plans, Volume 1.* Tulsa: PennWell Publishing Co., 1982.

8. ——*Dental Office Plans, Volume 2.* Tulsa: PennWell Publishing Co., 1985.

9. Two package libraries from the library service of the American Dental Association are most informative: *Practice Valuation, No. 4* and *Managed Care, No. 2.* Chicago: ADA Library Service, 211 East Chicago Avenue, #200, Chicago, Il 60611

# APPENDIX 4

# STATE AND REGIONAL DENTAL EXAMINING BOARDS

The following addresses are maintained by the American Association of Dental Examiners, 211 E. Chicago Ave., Chicago, IL 60611 (312) 440-7464, and are used here with permission of the Association. Information about national dental exams can be obtained from the Joint Commission on National Dental Examinations, American Dental Association, 211 E. Chicago Ave., Chicago, IL 60611; (312) 440-2678.

**State Board of Dental Examiners of Alabama**
Ms. Dianne E. Pool
Administrative Secretary
2308-B Starmount Circle
Huntsville, 35801
205/533-4638

**State of Alaska Board of Dental Examiners**
Ms. Carol Whelan
Administrator
Department of Commerce and Economic Dev.
P.O. Box 110806
Juneau, 99811-0806
907/465-2542

**Arizona State Board of Dental Examiners**
    Mr. Mark K. Steinberg
    Executive Director
    5060 N. 19th Ave. #406
    Phoenix, 85015
    602/255-3696

**Arkansas State Board of Dental Examiners**
    Ms. Judith Safly
    Executive Director
    Suite 1200
    323 Center Street
    Little Rock, 72201
    501/682-2085

**State of California Board of Dental Examiners**
    Ms. Georgetta Coleman
    Executive Officer
    1432 Howe Avenue, Suite 85B
    Sacramento, 95825
    916/263-2292

**Colorado State Board of Dental Examiners**
    Ms. Rosemary McCool
    Program Administrator
    1560 Broadway, Suite 1310
    Denver, 80202
    303/894-7758

**Connecticut Dental Commission**
    Ms. Debra Tomassone
    Board Liaison
    Medical Quality Assurance Division
    Connecticut Department of Health Services
    150 Washington St.
    Hartford, 06106
    203/566-4068

**Delaware State Board of Dental Examiners**
> Mrs. Sheila Wolfe
> Administrative Assistant
> P.O. Box 1401
> O'Neill Building
> Dover, 19903
> 302/739-4522

**District of Columbia Board of Dental Examiners**
> Ms. Shirley McLean-Fludd
> Contact Representative
> Department of Consumer and Regulatory Affairs
> 614 H. Street, NW, Room 904
> Washington, D.C. 20001
> 202/727-7478

**Florida Board of Dentistry**
> Mr. William H. Buckhalt
> Executive Director
> North Center
> 1940 N. Monroe St.
> Tallahassee, 32399-0765
> 904/488-6015

**Georgia Board of Dentistry**
> Dr. Frederick Meadows
> Executive Director
> 166 Pryor St. SW
> Atlanta, 30303
> 404-656-3925

**Hawaii State Board of Dental Examiners**
> Ms. Connie Cabral
> Executive Director
> Department of Commerce & Consumer Affairs
> P.O. Box 3469
> Honolulu, 96801
> 808/586-2702

**Idaho State Board of Dentistry**
 Ms. Sylvia Boyle
 Administrator
 Statehouse Mail
 Boise, 83720-6000
 208/334-2369

**Illinois State Board of Dentistry**
 Ms. Mary Wright
 Board Liaison
 Department of Professional Regulation
 320 W. Washington, 3rd Floor
 Springfield, 62786
 217/785-0872

**Indiana State Board of Dental Examiners**
 Ms. Barbara M. McNutt
 Director
 Health Professional Bureau
 402 W. Washington, Room 041
 Indianapolis, 46204
 317/233-4406

**Iowa State Board of Dental Examiners**
 Mrs. Constance L. Price
 Executive Director
 Executive Hills West
 1209 East Court
 Des Moines, 50319
 515/281-5157

**Kansas Dental Board**
 Ms. Carol L. Macdonald
 Administrative Secretary
 3601 SW 29th St., Suite 134
 Topeka, 66614
 913/273-0780

*Appendix 5*

**Kentucky Board of Dentistry**
Mr. Gary Munsie
Executive Director
2106 Bardstown Road
Louisville, 40205
502/451-6832

**Louisiana State Board of Dentistry**
C. Barry Ogden, Esq.
Executive Director
1515 Poydras Street
Suite 1850
New Orleans, 70112
504/568-8574

**Maine Board of Dental Examiners**
Ms. Irene Boucher
Executive Secretary
2 Bangor Street
State House Station 143
Augusta, 04333
207/287-3333

**Maryland State Board of Dental Examiners**
Mr. Larrie Bennett
Administrator
Metro-Executive Center
4201 Patterson Ave.
Baltimore, 21215-2299
410/764-4730

**Massachusetts Board of Registration in Dentistry**
Ms. Janet Selwitz, RDH, CDA
Assistant Secretary
100 Cambridge St., Room 1514
Boston, 02202
617/727-9928

**Michigan Board of Dentistry**
    Ms. Doris Foley
    Licensing Administrator
    Department of Commerce-BOPR
    P.O. Box 30018
    Lansing, 48909
    517/335-0918

**Minnesota Board of Dentistry**
    Mr. Richard Diercks
    Executive Director
    2700 University Ave., W., Suite 70
    St. Paul, 55114-1055
    621/642-0579

**Mississippi State Board of Dental Examiners**
    Ms. Annerin Long
    Licensing Board Administrator
    580 Springridge Road, Suite C
    P.O. Box 1960
    Clinton, 39060
    601/924-9622

**Missouri Dental Board**
    Mr. Alden Henrickson
    Executive Director
    P.O. Box 1367
    Jefferson City, 65102
    314/751-0040

**Montana Board of Dentistry**
    Ms. Lisa F. Casman
    Administrator
    111 N. Jackson
    Arcade Building, PO Box 200513
    Helena, 59620-0513
    406/444-3745

*Appendix 5*

**Nebraska Board of Examiners in Dentistry**
Ms. Becky Wisell
Board Coordinator
301 Centennial Mall South
P.O. Box 95007
Lincoln, 68509-5007
402/471-2115

**Nevada State Board of Dental Examiners**
Dr. William L. Thomason
Executive Secretary
4535 W. Sahara Ave., Number 108
Las Vegas, 89102
702/362-8993

**New Hampshire Board of Dental Examiners**
Dr. Raymond J. Jarvis
Executive Secretary
2 Industrial Park Dr.
Concord, 03301-8520
603/271-4561

**New Jersey State Board of Dentistry**
Ms. Agnes Clarke
Executive Director
124 Halsey St.
P.O. Box 45005
Newark, 07101
201/504-6405

**New Mexico Board of Dentistry**
Ms. Karen Valdex
Administrator
P.O. Drawer 8397
Sante Fe, 87504-8397
505/827-7165

**New York State Board For Dentistry**
 Dr. Martin A. Rubin
 Cultural Education Center, Room 3023
 Albany, 12230
 518/474-3838

**North Carolina State Board of Dental Examiners**
 Mrs. Christine H. Lockwood
 Executive Director
 3716 National Drive, Suite 221
 P.O. Box 32270
 Raleigh, 27622-2270
 919/781-4901

**North Dakota Board of Dentistry**
 Dr. Robert B. McKibben
 Box 179
 Valley City, 58071
 701/845-3708

**Ohio State Dental Board**
 Mr. Omar P. Whisman
 Executive Director
 77 S. High St., 18th Floor
 Columbus, 43266-0306
 614/466-2580

**Oklahoma Board of Governors Of Registered Dentists**
 Ms. Linda C. Campbell
 2726 N. Oklahoma Ave.
 Oklahoma City, 73105
 405/521-2350

**Oregon Board of Dentistry**
 Ms. Betty Reynolds
 Executive Director
 1515 SW Fifth Ave.
 Suite 400
 Portland, 97201
 503/229-5520

**Pennsylvania State Board of Dentistry**
Ms. June L. Barner
Administrative Assistant
P.O. Box 2649
Harrisburg, 17105
717/783-7162

**Puerto Rico Board of Dental Examiners**
Mr. Carlos Santana Rabell
Director, Examining Boards
Department of Health
Call Box 10200
San Juan, 00908
809/725-8161

**Rhode Island State Board of Examiners in Dentistry**
Mr. Robert W. McClanaghan
Administrator
3 Capitol Hill, Room 404
Providence, 02908-5097
401/277-2151

**South Carolina State Board of Dentistry**
Mr. H. Rion Alvey
Executive Director
1315 Blanding St.
Columbia, 29201
803/734-8904

**South Dakota State Board of Dentistry**
Ms. Anita Aker
Staff Assistant
P.O. Box 8047
Rapid City, 57709-8047
605-342-3026

**Tennessee Board of Dentistry**
Ms. Kaye Snell
Director
283 Plus Park Blvd.
Nashville, 37247-1010
614/367-6228

**Texas State Board of Dental Examiners**
Mr. C. Thomas Camp
Executive Director
333 Guadalupe, Tower 3, Suite 3800
Austin, 78701
512/463-6400

**Utah Board of Dentists And Dental Hygienists**
Ms. Diane Blake
Bureau Manager
Division of Occupation and Professional Licensing
P.O. Box 45805
Salt Lake City, 84145-0805

**Vermont State Board of Dental Examiners**
Ms. Diane LaFaille
Staff Assistant/Exec. Sec.
Secretary of State's Office
109 State St.
Montpelier, 05609-1106
802/828-2390

**Virginia Board of Dentistry**
Ms. Marcia J. Miller
Executive Director
6606 W. Broad St., 4th Fl.
Richmond, 23230-1717
804/662-9906

**Virgin Islands Board of Dental Examiners**
   Mrs. Jane Aubain
   Office Manager
   Department of Health
   48 Sugar Estate
   St. Thomas, 00802
   809/774-0017

**Washington Dental Health Care Boards**
   Ms. Susan Shoblom
   Executive Director
   P.O. Box 47867
   Olympia, 98504-7867
   206/753-2461

**West Virginia Board of Dental Examiners**
   Mr. James G. Anderson III
   P.O. Drawer 1459
   Beckley, 25802-1459
   304/252-8266

**Wisconsin Dentistry Examining Board**
   Mr. Patrick D. Braatx
   Administrator
   P.O. Box 8935
   1400 E. Washington Ave.
   Madison, 53708
   608/266-0483

**Wyoming Board of Dental Examiners**
   Ms. Shirley Thomas
   Executive Secretary
   P.O. Box 1270
   Powell, 82435
   307/754-7476

## REGIONAL DENTAL EXAMINING BOARDS

### Central Regional Dental Testing Service, Inc. (CRDTS)
Ms. Cynthia G. Barrett
Administrative Secretary
1725 Gage Blvd.
Topeka, KS 66604
913/273-0380

### Northeast Regional Board of Dental Examiners, Inc. (NERB)
Dr. William K. Collins
4645 Burroughs Ave., NE
3rd Floor
Washington, D.C. 20019
202/398-6196

### Southern Regional Testing Agency, Inc. (SRTA)
Mr. Robert W. Minnich
303 - 34th St., Suite 7
Virginia Beach, VA 23451
804/428-1003

### Western Regional Examining Board (WREB)
Ms. Linda Paul
Executive Administrator
10040 N. 25th Ave., #116
Phoenix, AZ 85021
602/944-3315

# INDEX

## A

Accountants, 50, 93, 106, 107, 111
   as Negotiator, 130
   Role in practice purchase, 131
   and Tax law, 106, 130
Accounts receivable, 114
ADA (American Dental Association) 14, 15, 97, 98
   Loan program, 126
   Managed care contract analysis, 159
   Unit work value concept, 167
ADA (Americans with Disabilities Act), 48
Advertising,
   Internal, 88
   Mall, 48,
   Practice broker, 68
   Realtor, 58,
   Space for lease, 60, 61
   Specialist, 24,
   Visibility, 25, 27

Advertisement, newspaper, locating lease, 58
Agent, real estate, buyer's 65,
   Expertise, 36
   Leasing, 25
   Loan source, 64
   as Negotiator, 62
Analyzing assets, 104-107, 109, 112
Annual statement, 80
Appraisal, practice broker's, 99, 100, 118
Assets, financial, 64, 119
Assets, emotional, 9,
Assets, practice,
   Accounts receivable, 114
   Analyzing, 104-109, 112
   as Collateral, 121, 127
   Corporate, 111
   Managed care contract, 83
   Patient as, 98
   Value of inactive office, 117
   and Space sharing, 146

and Taxes in practice sale, 130
Assistants,
    as Advisors, 46
    Importance to seller's practice, 71-72
    Knowledge of seller's practice, 72
    Loyalty to seller, 74
    Resenting buyer, 92
    Rural practice, 32
    Space sharing problems, 142, 146
    and Practice continuity, 76
    and Salary cuts by buyer, 92
Associate, contribution to goodwill, 136-137
Attorney, 61, 111
    as Negotiator, 62, 130
    and/or Accountant, 50
    and Managed care contract, 159
    and Purchasing practice with B

## B

building, 116, 131
    and Real estate, 66
    and Taxes, 106
    and Title insurance, 65
Banker, 120, 122
    Loan requirements, 64, 107-108, 113, 123
    Real estate advisor, 36, 127
    and Leasehold loans, 49
    and Property values, 38
Bosworth, 166, 170
Broker, practice,
    Advantages of using, 68
    Advertising, 68
    Buyer's consultant, 69
    Contract, 131
    Ethics of, 69

Locating a, 68
Negotiator, 130
Qualifications, 70
and Appraisal, 99, 100, 118
and Financing, 126
and Prospectus, 45, 79
Broker, real estate, 57
    as Buyer's agent, 65
Builder, 176
Buyer, practice,
    as Associate, 115, 137
    /Broker relationship, 69
    Escrow, 131
    Group practice, 116
    Loan default, 121, 133
    Loan rate, 121-122
    Non-competition clause, 131-133
    Relationship with seller, 139
    Relative practice value to, 108
    Seller as landlord, 117
    Seller's responsibility in partner ship, 136
    and Appraisal, 108
    and Equipment sale/leaseback, 127
    and Negotiation, 129
    and Special practice situations, 110
Buyer, real estate, 36, 66, 131
Buyer's agent/broker, 65

## C

Capitation, 152-153
Closing costs, 112-113, 120, 124, 127
Collateral, 121, 127
Contract,
    Broker's standard, 131
    Employment leading to buyout, 137, 138
    Goodwill value in, 136

HMO/PPO,
    Effect on Gross income, 80
    Master contract, 160
    Negotiation, 150
    Risk assignment, 151, 158-161
Insurance, ideal, 152
Interim agreement, 131
Linking real estate to practice, 132
Non-competition clause in, 131-133
Partnership, 138
Practice purchase, 131
Contractor, 58, 65

## D

Decisions, emotional, IX
Depreciation, 7, 84

## E

Emotional assets, 8-9
Equipment,
    Depreciation, 7, 84
    Installation, 54
    Leasing, 127
    Practice purchase, condition in, 67, 68
    Purchasing, 54-55, 105
    Sale/leaseback, 127
    Space requirements, 53-55
    Space sharing, 141, 145
    Usefulness, 67-68, 106
    Valuing, 104-105, 108, 124, 137
    and Fee structure, 169, 173
Ethics, practice broker, 69

## F

Fair market value, 107-108
Family considerations, 12
Fee-for-service, 4, 153, 163

Patient's insurance covering, 151, 152, 154-155, 162
PPO imitating, 156
Role in fee analysis, 167, 173
and Appraisal, 80
Fees,
    ADA unit value, 167
    Capitation, 152-153
    Components of, 169-172
    History of, 165-167
    Perception of quality, 26-27
    PPO schedules, 152-153
    Profitability of, 167-168, 172
    Public questioning of, 3
    Seating charge, 154
    Simplified determination of, 172
    Supplementary in managed care, 153
    Total charge per patient, 100
    and Efficiency, 82
    and Laboratory charges, 165
    and Insurance co-payment, 153
    and Managed care, 83
    and Type of practice, 44
Female practitioner, 8, 36
Financial statement, 64, 108
    Importance to seller, 126
    and Loan package, 122

## G

Goodwill,
    Accounts receivable, 114
    Allocation of, 106. 136
    Associate's contribution to, 136-137
    Determining, 107-108, 110
    Main ingredient, 76
    Reducing valuation, 106, 117
    Value listed in sales contract, 136

and Emergency sale, 117
and Lenders, 125

# H

HMO, (also see :Managed care" and "Contract")
    Definition, 152-153
    Contracting with, 4, 29
    Government sponsorship, 155
    Hybrids, 153
    and Cost shifting, 163
    and Loan application, 125
    and Practice appraisal, 109
    and Practice gross, 80
HMO/PPO contract,
    Effect on Gross income, 80
    Master contract, 160
    Negotiation of, 150
    Risk assignment in, 151, 158, 159, 161
Hygienists,
    as Advisors, 46
    Profitability of, 87, 172
    Rural practice, 32

# J

JADA, 69

# L

LEAAPAET, 153-154
Lease,
    Availability of space, 23
    Detailed, 48
    Investigating area near, 26, 62
    Negotiating, 62-63
    Renewing, 62
    Standard 61
    Termination, 49, 59
    Terms, 48, 49, 59-61
    Transferability of, 105, 125
    and Practice purchase, 117
    and Realtors, 36
    and Remodeling, 35, 49, 58
    and Security service, 25
    and Space sharing, 145
Lease/purchase, 50
Leasehold improvements, value of, 105-107
Leasehold loans, 49
Leasing,
    Agent, 25
    Compared to buying, 47
    Desirability of malls/strip centers, 28
    Equipment, 111, 127
    Flexibility of, 51-52
    Janitor service, 48
    Locating property to, 57
    to Yourself, 50
LEAT, 153, 154
Loan,
    ADA program, 126
    Adverse terms, 120, 122
    Alternate sources, 126
    Default, 121, 133
    Goodwill value in, 125
    HMO considerations, 125
    Initiating, 122, 124
    Rate, 121-122,
    Realtor as source, 64
    Remodeling, 49,
    Requirements, 64, 108, 109, 114-115, 119
    Second mortgage, 121
    and Location, 36

Location, general considerations,
    Central/suburban, 29
    Economics of, 14-20
    Fees, 26,
    General practitioner, 24-28, 31
    Importance of, 12
    Mall, 29
    Managed care, 27, 149, 161
    Medical center, 27
    Negatives of owning, 51
    Parking, 30
    Personal considerations, 12-14
    Purchasing, 52
    Residential subdivisions, 31
    Restrictions, community, 36
    Rural, 30-33
    Small town, 52
    Specialist, 24, 27
    Strip center, 29
    Trends, economic and social, 35, 36
    Type of practice, 11, 37, 42
    and Practice purchase, 70-71, 107
    and State board, 13
Location, urban/central,
    Purchasing building, 47

# M

Mall,
    advertising, 48
    Definition, 29
    Dental offices in, 29, 60-61
    Services provided in, 48
    Suburban business center, 29
Managed care, (also see "HMO" and "PPO")
    ADA contract analysis, 159
    Contract stability, 160
    Definition, 143
    Dentist's attitude toward, 164
    Future of, 163
    Negotiating position when joining, 150-151
    Opinion regarding joining, 150
    Patients, mixing with traditional, 164
    Patient attitude toward, 162
    Percentage patients covered, 162
    Supplementary fee, 154
    Variations of, 156
    and Government, 155
    and Location, 27
    and Patient load, 160
    and Patient treatment, 159, 160
    and Profitability, 169
Minority, 9, 110

# N

Net worth, 119
Negotiator, 64, 130
Non-competition clause, 131-132, 137

# O

OSHA, 25, 95, 169

# P

Partnership,
    Contract, 138-139
    Control of, 116
    Incremental purchase of, 116, 135
    Purchase alternatives, 67,
    Suburban, 29
    Within space sharing, 145
PPO, (also see "HMO" and "Managed care")
    Combined with HMO, 154
    Effect on income, 80, 157, 161, 173
    Fee schedule, 152-153
    Imitating fee-for-service, 156

Mechanism, 152
　　　and Loan information, 125, 153
Patients as assets, 98
Politics, intra-office, 73, 142, 146
Practice analysis 70, 79, 84-86, 113
Practice purchase agreement, 132
Practice value to buyer, 104
Pro-forma, 114, 124
Prospectus, 45, 79
Property value, 38

# R

Realtor/broker, advertising, 58
Reserve account, 85
Rural, (also see "Small town")
　　Appearance, 39
　　Checking location, 37
　　Practice purchase contract, 133
　　Statistical considerations, 43, 98

# S

Sale lease/back, 127
Satellite office, 45
Seating charge, 154
Second mortgage, 121
Seller, practice, 83, 96, 97
　　as Lessor, 17
　　Alternative sales arrangements, 66, 121
　　Assistants, 71-73, 76
　　Attitude, 68, 76, 81, 110, 131
　　Death of, 138
　　Fee schedule, 165
　　Group practice, 115
　　Liabilities, 93, 111
　　Overhead, 113
　　Reasons for sale, 45
　　Retaining in practice, 67, 116
　　Sale price, 103-104, 117
　　Selling office location, 116
　　Taxes, 107, 130
　　and Broker, 69
　　and Financing, 103, 112, 132
　　and Non-competition clause, 137
　　and "Out" clause, 137
Seller, real estate, 36
Small town,
　　Advantages, 33
　　Assessing, 31-32
　　Becoming suburb, 28
　　Costs, 32
　　Definition, 31
　　Dental insurance in, 162
　　Ethnic, 110
　　Financial assistance in, 33, 127
　　Hygienist in, 32
　　Life style, 14
　　Office location, 32
　　Owning office in, 51-52,
　　Practice type, 33
　　Satellite office, 45
　　Zoning, 32
Space requirements, office, 53-54, 55
Space sharing,
　　Advantages, 142
　　Assets, 145
　　Assistants resenting, 142, 146
　　Fairness in, 146
　　Hazards 142
　　Joint ownership of equipment, 145
　　Leading to partnership, 147
　　Lease considerations, 145
　　Partnership within, 145
　　Practice alternative, 67
　　Staff, 147
Specialist,
　　Advertising, 24
　　Competition, 45

Decor, 50
Location, 24, 27
Referrals, 24
Role in managed care, 158
Rural availability, 30
Satellite office, 45
Spouse 4, 12
    Credit standing, 122, 123, 125-126
    Role in community, 43
    Role in office, 96, 146
Strip center,
    Advantages/disadvantages, 29-30, 61
    Definition, 29
    Dental office in, 29-30
    Locating in new, 58
    Services provided, 48
Suburb,
    Choosing location in, 30
    Definition, 27, 29
    Development of, 28, 29
Suburban,
    Central business district, 28, 29
    Homogenous, 28
    Hospitals, 27
    Location advantages, 26-27
    Parking, 30

# T

Tax law, 106, 130
Title insurance, 65
Trends, economic, 15

# U

Utility restrictions, 25, 35

# V

Value,
    Goodwill, 106, 117
    Inactive practice, 109
    Practice to buyer, 108

# Z

Zoning, 30-31, 51